THE JOURNAL OF
SUSTAINABLE MOBILITY
Volume 2 Issue 1

June 2015

Special Issue: **Sustainable Mobility in China and its Implications for Emerging Economies**

Guest Editors: Fuquan Zhao and Han Hao, Tsinghua University, China
Michael Zhang, Nottingham Trent University, UK

© 2015 Greenleaf Publishing Limited.
All written material, unless otherwise stated, is the copyright of Greenleaf
Publishing Limited. Views expressed in articles and letters are those of the
contributors, and not necessarily those of the publisher.

Cover image credits:
'Star Ferry Hong Kong' by Leon Brocard is licensed under CC BY 2.0. 'Canadian Pacific
Train' by Steve Jurvetson is licensed under CC BY 2.0. The full license can be found at:
https://creativecommons.org/licenses/by/2.0/legalcode

print ISSN 2059-1578   *online* ISSN 2053-2350

THE JOURNAL OF SUSTAINABLE MOBILITY

Editor-in-Chief Michael Zhang,
Reader in International Strategy at Nottingham Business School, Nottingham Trent University, UK

Publisher Anna Comerford, Greenleaf Publishing, UK
Production Editor Sadie Gornall-Jones, Greenleaf Publishing, UK

CONSULTING EDITORS

Professor Baback Yazdani, Dean of Nottingham Business School, Nottingham Trent University, UK

Professor Francis Assadian, Director of Automotive Mechatronics Centre, Cranfield University, UK

Dr Paul Nieuwenhuis, Cardiff Business School, UK

AREA EDITOR FOR TECHNOLOGY AND ENGINEERING

Dr Stefano Longo, Department of Automotive Engineering, Cranfield University, UK

AREA EDITOR FOR TRANSPORT MANAGEMENT SYSTEMS

Dr Evtim Peytchev, School of Science and Technology, Nottingham Trent University, UK

AREA EDITOR FOR CORPORATE GOVERNANCE

Professor Hong Zhao, Deputy Dean, School of Management, Graduate University of Chinese Academy of Sciences, China

REGIONAL EDITOR FOR CHINA AND THE ASIA PACIFIC

Professor Lingling Zhang, School of Management, Graduate University of Chinese Academy of Sciences, China

AREA EDITOR FOR TECHNOLOGY

Dr James Njuguna, Institute for Innovation, Design & Sustainability, School of Engineering, Robert Gordon University, UK

BOOK REVIEW EDITOR

Dr Hafez Abdo, School of Management, Nottingham Business School, UK

The Journal of Sustainable Mobility is an online only publication, though print copies may be produced for certain events. *The Journal of Sustainable Mobility* is included in both the Sustainable Organization Library (SOL) collection and in the smaller Greenleaf Online Library (GOL). See www.gseresearch.com/sol for further information.

CORRESPONDENCE

The Journal of Sustainable Mobility encourages response from its readers to any of the issues raised in the journal. All correspondence is welcomed and should be sent to the General Editor c/o Greenleaf Publishing, Aizlewood's Mill, Nursery St, Sheffield S3 8GG, UK; jsm@greenleaf-publishing.com.

All content should be submitted via **online submission**. For more information see the journal homepage at www.greenleaf-publishing.com/jsm.

Books to be considered for review should be marked for the attention of the Book Review Editor c/o Greenleaf Publishing, Aizlewood's Mill, Nursery St, Sheffield S3 8GG, UK; jsm@greenleaf-publishing.com.

• All articles published in *The Journal of Sustainable Mobility* are assessed by an external panel of business professionals, consultants and academics.

SUBSCRIPTION RATES

The Journal of Sustainable Mobility is published twice annually, appearing in Spring and Autumn of each year. Subscription rates for organizations are £540.00/€650.00/US$850.00 for one year (two issues) and for individuals £80.00/€112.00/US$150.00. Cheques should be made payable to Greenleaf Publishing and sent to:

The Journal of Sustainable Mobility
Greenleaf Publishing Ltd, Aizlewood Business Centre, Aizlewood's Mill, Nursery Street, Sheffield S3 8GG, UK
Tel: +44 (0)114 282 3475   Fax: +44 (0)114 282 3476   Email: jsm@greenleaf-publishing.com.
Or order from our website: www.greenleaf-publishing.com/jsm.

ADVERTISING

The Journal of Sustainable Mobility will accept a strictly limited amount of display advertising in future issues. It will also be possible to book inserts. Suitable material for promotion includes publications, conferences and consulting services. For details on rates and availability, please email jsm@greenleaf-publishing.com.

The Journal of Sustainable Mobility is published in partnership with

Editorial

Sustainable Mobility in China from a Global Perspective

Volume 2 Issue 1 *June 2015*

Michael Zhang
Nottingham Trent University, UK

READING THE NEWLY PUBLISHED Synthesis Report (SYR) on Climate Change 2014 by the Intergovernmental Panel on Climate Change (IPCC, 2015), it becomes clear that there is increasing scientific evidence of anthropogenic impact, i.e. influence of human activities, on global climate change. Of particular concern are the continued increases of CO_2 emissions and CO_2 concentration in the atmosphere. The SYR notes that 'CO_2 concentrations are increasing at the fastest observed decadal rate of change (2.0 ± 0.1 ppm/yr) for 2002–2011' (ibid.: 44). This reflects our summary of the changes of CO_2 concentrations using previous IPCC and IEA data (Zhang and Yazdani, 2014). The magnitude of annual CO_2 emissions was 30.3 gigatonnes in 2010 and the level of CO_2 concentration reached 400 parts per million (ppm) in 2013 (IEA, 2012; IPCC, 2013). Over the period of 23 years between 1990 and 2013 the level of CO_2 concentration rose from 353 ppm to 400 ppm giving it an average

annual increase of 2.04 ppm/yr. If this trend remains unchanged CO_2 concentration will by circa 2037 have reached the level of 450 ppm which is the baseline of CO_2 concentration stabilisation used by many researchers for modelling global climate change. The IPCC experts estimate with high confidence that about 50% of the cumulative CO_2 emissions generated by human activities during the industrial period between 1750 and 2011 occurred in the last 40 years (IPCC, 2015: 45). Indeed, in the last 30 years or so the world has witnessed marked changes in the contributions of CO_2 emissions by some leading nations. As the leading industrialised country the US had been the largest CO_2 emission contributor until 2007, when it was overtaken by China. In 1980 the US contributed 25.8% of the 18.0 gigatonnes of world CO_2 emissions. In comparison, in the same year China's contribution of CO_2 emissions accounted for only 7.9% as shown in Table 1 (IEA, 2012).

Table 1 CO_2 emissions from selected countries/regions 1980–2010 (million tonnes)

Source: IEA, 2012

	1980		1990		2000		2010	
	Total	%	Total	%	Total	%	Total	%
China	1,420	7.9	2,244	10.7	3,077	13.1	7,259	24.0
USA	4,662	25.8	4,869	23.2	5,698	24.2	5,369	17.7
EU27	n/a	n/a	4,050	19.3	3,831	16.3	3,660	12.1
World	18,042	100	20,974	100	23,509	100	30,276	100

In 1990 the total world CO_2 emissions rose to 21.0 gigatonnes, of which the US contributed 23.2% and China 10.7%. EU15, a collective body of 15 European countries before 2004, contributed 19.3% in 1990. The following two decades saw three clear trends emerging: (1) continued reduction of CO_2 emissions in the EU15 then and now EU27; (2) slightly fluctuating with overall decrease of CO_2 emissions in the US; and (3) significant increase of CO_2 emissions in China. As a result, reduction of CO_2 emissions in China has become a priority in the national policy agenda, as Zhao, Hao and Zhang argue in the Guest Editorial of this Special Issue.

The global transport sector in general is the second largest contributor to total CO_2 emissions. In EU27 countries CO_2 emissions from the transport sector accounted for 24.3% in 2012, below that from the energy sector at 29.2% (European Commission, 2012). Particularly important is the annual change of CO_2 emissions over the 1990 level. Categorically all sectors (including energy, industry, residential and commercial) but transport have seen to various degrees reduction in CO_2 emissions from 1990 to 2012 (ibid.). This pattern was formed in the context of stabilisation of vehicle ownership of 567 vehicles per 1,000 people in EU27 in 2010 (Ward's, 2013). In stark contrast, vehicle ownership in China was merely 58 vehicles per 1,000 people in 2010. As a result, CO_2 emissions from China's transport sector accounted for only 7.5% of the total 7,259 million tonnes in 2010, far below the world average 22.3% and the significantly higher rate of 30.2% registered for the US as shown in Table 2.

Table 2 CO_2 emissions from the transport sector in selected countries/regions 2010 (million tonnes)

Source: IEA, 2012

	Total (A)	%	Transport (B)	% (B/A)	Road transport (C)	% (C/B)
China	7,259	24.0	546	7.5	401	73.4
US	5,369	17.7	1,621	30.2	1,401	86.4
EU27	3,660	12.1	900	24.6	848	94.2
World	30,276	100.0	6,756	22.3	4,972	73.6

The development of China's transport systems in general and the road transport system in particular, with its large potential contribution to CO_2 emissions in the coming two decades or so, i.e. 2015–2035, demands a special forum of investigation and discussion, and therefore the resultant presentation of this Special Issue (SI) dedicated to the subject. I thank the Guest Editors, Professor Fuquan Zhao and Dr Han Hao from Tsinghua University for their effort and commitment to collecting and editing the papers included in this SI. The contributions to the SI provide a wide range of topics with in-depth analysis of the complex transport systems in China. I hope that the findings from this SI will shed light on our debate and examination of sustainable mobility with special reference to large developing countries.

References

European Commission (2012). *Reducing emissions from transport*. European Commission website at http://ec.europa.eu/clima/policies/transport/index_en.htm accessed on 10 April 2015.

IEA (2012). *CO2 Emissions from Fuel Combustion*, IEA Statistics, International Energy Agency, Paris.

IPCC (2013). *Climate Change 2013: The Physical Science Basis*. Contribution of Working Group I to the Fifth Assessment Report of the Intergovernmental Panel on Climate Change, Cambridge University Press, Cambridge, UK.

IPCC (2015). *Climate Change 2014: Synthesis Report. Contribution of Working Groups I, II and III to the Fifth Assessment Report of the Intergovernmental Panel on Climate Change*. IPCC, Geneva, Switzerland.

Ward's (2013). *World vehicle in use dataset 2006-2010*. Wardsauto Data Center, at http://wardsauto.com/data-browse-world accessed on 20 May 2013.

Zhang, M. and Yazdani, B. (2014). Paradigm Change of Mobility in the Twenty-first Century. *Journal of Sustainable Mobility* 1, 9-18.

Dr **Michael Zhang** is Reader in International Strategy at Nottingham Business School, Nottingham Trent University. He teaches core modules of International Business and Strategic Management at both undergraduate and postgraduate levels. His research interest covers the following areas: (1) economic development and market process; (2) technology analysis and entrepreneurship; and (3) corporate sustainability and organisational learning. Before his academic career, Michael worked in the automotive industry and was involved in international technological transfer programmes. He has work experience in China, Japan and the UK and speaks Chinese, English and Japanese. Michael has published in a range of economic and management journals, *inter alia*: the *International Journal of Technology Management, International Small Business Journal, Journal of the Asian Pacific Economy, R&D Management, Technology Analysis & Strategic Management*. He served a term of three years, 2011–13, as a member of the Editorial Review Board of the *Journal of International Business Studies*. He was a guest editor for a Special Issue of the *International Journal of Entrepreneurship and Innovation* in 2012. In July 2013 he successfully launched, and became the founding Editor-in-Chief of, a new peer-reviewed journal: the *Journal of Sustainable Mobility* with Greenleaf Publishing.

✉ Nottingham Business School, Nottingham Trent University, Burton Street, Nottingham NG1 4BU, UK

🖳 michael.zhang@ntu.ac.uk

Guest Editorial

Sustainable Mobility in China and its Implications for Emerging Economies

Volume 2 Issue 1 *June 2015*

Fuquan Zhao
Tsinghua University, China

Han Hao
Tsinghua University, China

Michael Zhang
Nottingham Trent University, UK

DRIVEN BY RAPID ECONOMIC GROWTH and urbanisation, China's transport sector underwent profound changes over recent years, with mass motorisation as one of its major characteristics. China's vehicle stock grew from 16 million in 2000 to 154 million in 2014, implying an annual growth rate of 17.5%, which is comparable to the highest growth rates of developed countries during the same historical period (National Bureau of Statistics, 2014). The rapid growth of vehicle ownership raises concerns over several issues, including urban traffic congestion, energy security, air pollution and climate change. In Beijing, vehicles were responsible for 31.1% of PM2.5 emissions from local sources, topping any other single source (Beijing Municipal Environmental Protection Bureau, 2014). China's transport-associated CO_2 emissions accounted for about 8% of total CO_2 emissions from fuel combustion in 2011, and is increasing faster than any other sectors (IEA, 2013). Recent research suggests that energy consumption and greenhouse gases (GHG) emissions from China's transport sector are likely to keep increasing through 2030 (Development Research Center of the State Council, 2009). How to establish a sustainable mobility system is one of the greatest challenges China faces.

From a scientific research perspective, there is an urgent need to understand the underlying reasons and dynamics behind changes in China's transport sector, identifying key challenges and opportunities in addressing the emerging issues, and developing strategies and roadmaps to achieve the target of sustainable mobility (Zhang and Yazdani, 2014). In this special issue of the *Journal of Sustainable Mobility*, we have included four original research articles, which address the above-mentioned issues from the perspectives of urban transport structure, suburban transport, advanced vehicle market diffusion, and eco-efficiency assessment of automotive products, respectively. As the current transportation issues in China share significant similarity with other large developing countries, we hope the insights into China's sustainable mobility will shed some light on the common issues other developing countries encounter.

The tremendous growth of vehicle stock has caused substantial changes in the transport system and structure. For instance, the share of vehicle travel out of total urban travel in Beijing increased from 23.2% in 2000 to 34.2% in 2014. During the same period, the share of non-motorized travel decreased from 41.5% to lower than 20% (Beijing Transportation Research Center, 2013). Infrastructure plays an essential role in determining transport structure. Since 2005, China has invested over 1 trillion yuan (US$161.3 billion at the 2013 exchange rate, World Bank) in the construction of urban rail infrastructure (Ministry of Housing and Urban-Rural Development, 2013). The total length of urban rail transit reached 2,408 km in 2013 (National Bureau of Statistics, 2014). Twenty cities have built bus rapid transit (BRT) systems, constituting a total operating length of over 540 km (Institute for Transportation and Development Policy, 2015). Many municipal governments in China have in recent years offered generous subsidies to public transport, maintaining the bus and rail tariffs at considerably low levels. With all these efforts, urban public transport, with urban rail as the representative, appears to be superseding vehicle use

growth and is more appropriate for the dense urban fabric and desirable to reduce energy consumption, air pollution and GHG emissions, as the paper by Gao, Newman and Webster in this issue concluded.

Suburban transport is another important part of the transport system, which has not been intensively studied by existing literatures. In the paper by Sun and Doulet in this issue, using community-based mobility services in Shanghai as a case, the authors shared their insights into the flexible and sustainable transport system for suburban China of 2050, with implications on intermodality, transformation of the institutional framework and new market segment for community-based transport.

Fuel economy is one of the essential factors determining energy and environmental impacts of the transport sector. In the early 2000s, China's vehicle fuel economy significantly lagged behind developed countries. The fleet average fuel economy of China's new passenger vehicles was 10% worse than those of Japan and Germany (Oliver et al., 2009). This situation has been largely improved after the implementation of China's fuel economy standards. China issued fuel economy standards for passenger vehicles, light duty commercial vehicles and heavy duty commercial vehicles in 2004, 2007 and 2011, respectively. The fleet average fuel consumption rate decreased from 8.16 L/100 km in 2006 to 7.31 L/100 km in 2013 (iCET, 2014), with the target of reaching 5 L/100 km in 2020. To encourage the purchase of fuel-efficient passenger vehicles, China set a lower purchase tax rate for passenger vehicles with displacement volumes of 1.6 L or lower from 2009 to 2010. Since 2010, purchases of fuel-efficient vehicles qualify for a 3000 yuan (US$483.9) subsidy. In 2009, the Chinese Government invested 5 billion yuan (US$806.5 million) in accelerating the scrappage of old, inefficient vehicles. However, as Hao et al. (2011b) argued, improving fuel economy alone is not enough to achieve the sustainable targets in China's transport sector.

The Chinese Government considers electric vehicles (EV) a priority among the advanced vehicle technologies. In the 'Industry Development Plan for Energy Saving and New Energy Vehicles', the accumulated sales of battery electric vehicles and plug-in hybrid electric vehicles were projected to reach 5 million in 2020 (Chinese State Council, 2012). To achieve this ambitious target, both the central and local governments have implemented a package of measures, including subsidising EV purchase and charging infrastructure construction, and purchase tax exemption, to promote EV market diffusion (Hao et al., 2014). By the end of 2014, 723 charging stations as well as nearly 29,000 charging posts have been built. However, EV sales are far lower than the announced targets, due largely to high vehicle cost, charging inconvenience, and range anxiety. The paper in this issue by Du, Chen, Gao and Ouyang analysed the key factors affecting EV market diffusion, which is of high relevance to both policy-makers and EV manufacturers.

With the rapid growth of China's automotive industry, its environmental and energy impacts are becoming more and more significant, which is of great concern to both researchers and policy-makers, home and abroad. However, existing studies in China's context have not established an integrated system of assessment of the socioeconomic impacts from the production and use of automotive products, making it difficult to achieve optimisation through the industrial chain from a global perspective. In particular, the software platforms for such assessments, which have already been widely used in the US and the EU such as the GREET Model (Wang, 2014), have not been well developed in China's context yet. In the paper by Yin, Chen, Yang, Xie and Liao in this issue, an eco-efficiency assessment system, 'Vehicle-IA system', for the automotive products in China was established, with the aim of guiding the automotive manufacturers to design and produce cars with better socioeconomic impacts.

China's efforts to establish a sustainable mobility system create an opportunity for researchers. Policies need to be developed in the context of China's unique administrative system, which cannot be well adapted by existing studies from developed countries. For example, mandatory policies play an essential role in China's transport policy system, such as the administrative restrictions on vehicle purchase and vehicle use, which have been implemented in many of China's large cities (Hao et al., 2011a). These policies have immediate effects on controlling transport demand. If designed properly, they can improve transport equity as well. However, they are not market-based and may cause overall inefficiency. Besides, these policies are often associated with low public acceptance. Research plays an extremely important role in evaluating such existing policies and raising recommendations for further improvements. There is large potential for researchers to participate in forming the strategy for sustainable mobility in China. The *Journal of Sustainable Mobility* will continue to serve as a platform for researchers, policy-makers and entrepreneurs to exchange ideas and promote the realisation of sustainable mobility through joint effort.

References

Beijing Municipal Environmental Protection Bureau, 2014. *PM2.5 Source Apportionment in Beijing*, Beijing.

Beijing Transportation Research Center, 2013. *Beijing Transportation Development Annual Report 2013*, Beijing.

Chinese State Council, 2012. *Industry Development Plan for Energy Saving and New Energy Vehicles*, Beijing.

Development Research Center of the State Council, 2009. *2050 China Energy and CO_2 Emissions Report*, Beijing.

Hao, H., Wang, H., Ouyang, M., 2011a. Comparison of policies on vehicle ownership and use between Beijing and Shanghai and their impacts on fuel consumption by passenger vehicles. *Energy Policy*, 39, 1016-1021.

Hao, H., Wang, H., Ouyang, M., 2011b. Fuel conservation and GHG (Greenhouse gas) emissions mitigation scenarios for China's passenger vehicle fleet. *Energy*, 36, 6520-6528.

Hao, H., Ou, X., Du, J., Wang, H., Ouyang, M., 2014. China's electric vehicle subsidy scheme: Rationale and impacts. *Energy Policy*, 73, 722-732.

iCET, 2014. *China Passenger Vehicle Fuel Consumption Development Annual Report*. Beijing.

IEA, 2013. *CO₂ Emissions from Fuel Combustion*, International Energy Agency, Paris.

Institute for Transportation and Development Policy, 2015. *Total Length of BRT Lane*, http://www.chinabrt.org (accessed March 20, 2015).

Ministry of Housing and Urban-Rural Development, 2013. *China Urban Construction Statistical Yearbook 2013*, Beijing.

National Bureau of Statistics, 2014. *China Statistical Yearbook 2000-2014*, Beijing.

Oliver, H.H., Gallagher, K.S., Tian, D., Zhang, J., 2009. China's fuel economy standards for passenger vehicles: Rationale, policy process, and impacts. *Energy Policy*, 37, 4720-4729.

Wang, M., 2014. *GREET.net 2014*, Argonne National Laboratory.

Zhang, M., and Yazdani, B., 2014. Paradigm Change of Mobility in the Twenty-first Century. *Journal of Sustainable Mobility* 1, 9-18.

Dr **Frank (Fuquan) Zhao** is a Professor and Director of the Automotive Strategy Research Institute at Tsinghua University, China, since May 2013. Dr Zhao has published five books and more than 300 academic papers, and owned more than 100 patents. Dr Zhao received many recognitions in his career including but not limited to: Fellow of SAE in 2006, China Automobile Industry Outstanding Person in 2008, CTO of the Year in 2008 and Executive of the Year for Product Planning in 2009 by China Automotive News, the Silver Medal of National Scientific and Technological Progress in 2009, the Gold Medal of China Automotive Science and Technology Progress in 2012, and the Gold Medal of China Enterprise Management in 2012.

✉ State Key Laboratory of Automotive Safety and Energy, Tsinghua University, Beijing 100084, China

🖳 zhaofuquan@tsinghua.edu.cn

Dr **Han Hao** is a research assistant at the Department of Automotive Engineering, Tsinghua University. He holds a doctoral degree and a bachelor degree both from the Department of Automotive Engineering, Tsinghua University. His research interests include China's automotive industry development strategy, automotive technology strategy, transport energy system modelling, and transport policy in the context of climate change.

✉ State Key Laboratory of Automotive Safety and Energy, Tsinghua University, Beijing 100084, China

🖳 hao@tsinghua.edu.cn

Dr **Michael Zhang** is Reader in International Strategy at Nottingham Business School, Nottingham Trent University. He teaches core modules of International Business and Strategic Management at both undergraduate and postgraduate levels. His research interest covers the following areas: (1) economic development and market process; (2) technology analysis and entrepreneurship; and (3) corporate sustainability and organisational learning. Before his academic career, Michael worked in the automotive industry and was involved in international technological transfer programmes. He has work experience in China, Japan and the UK and speaks Chinese, English and Japanese. Michael has published in a range of economic and management journals, *inter alia*: the *International Journal of Technology Management, International Small Business Journal, Journal of the Asian Pacific Economy, R&D Management, Technology Analysis & Strategic Management*. He served a term of three years, 2011–13, as a member of the Editorial Review Board of the *Journal of International Business Studies*. He was a guest editor for a Special Issue of the *International Journal of Entrepreneurship and Innovation* in 2012. In July 2013 he successfully launched, and became the founding Editor-in-Chief of, a new peer-reviewed journal: the *Journal of Sustainable Mobility* with Greenleaf Publishing.

✉ Nottingham Business School, Nottingham Trent University, Burton Street, Nottingham NG1 4BU, UK

🖳 michael.zhang@ntu.ac.uk

DOI: [10.9774/GLEAF.8757.2014.ju.00003]

Transport Transitions in Beijing

From Bikes to Automobiles to Trains

Yuan Gao, Peter Newman and Philip Webster

Curtin University Sustainability Policy (CUSP) Institute, Western Australia

Beijing is one of China's most significant cities and thus its transport transitions represent much of what is happening across all of China. This paper recognises three major transitions. The pre modern phase of the bicycle dominated Beijing from 1949 to 2001. With considerable economic development and a well-established automotive industry, Beijing experienced the Automobile phase from 2002 to 2010. This phase began to replace bicycles on Beijing's streets and led to major traffic congestion, air pollution and accidents. A third Train phase emerged in 2011 with the dramatic expansion of the Beijing Metro and associated bus systems as well as a formulated transportation demand management programme. Its growth now appears to be gradually transcending automobile use growth and is more appropriate for Beijing's dense urban fabric and desire to reduce its automobile carbon footprint.

- Transport transitions
- Beijing
- Urban fabrics
- Economic growth
- Administrative guidance
- Transport demand management

Yuan Gao is currently undertaking her PhD study at Curtin University Sustainability Policy (CUSP) Institute in Western Australia. The topic of her research is sustainable Chinese urban transport. She was a recipient of the Intergovernmental Panel on Climate Change (IPCC) Scholarship granted by the prestigious Prince Albert II of Monaco Foundation in 2014 and 2015.

Faculty of Humanities, Curtin University Sustainability Policy (CUSP) Institute, Building 209, 133 Kent Street, Curtin University Bentley Campus, Perth 6163, Australia

gaoyuan8416@hotmail.com

Peter Newman is the John Curtin Distinguished Professor of Sustainability at Curtin University. He has written 17 books on sustainable cities and sustainable transport. He was the Lead Author for Transport on the IPCC for its 5th Assessment Report. He was awarded the Order of Australia for his services to urban design and sustainable transport.

Faculty of Humanities, Curtin University Sustainability Policy (CUSP) Institute, Building 209, 133 Kent Street, Curtin University Bentley Campus, Perth 6163, Australia

p.newman@curtin.edu.au

Philip Webster works as a Research Assistant for the Curtin University Sustainability Policy (CUSP) Institute. He specialises in academic research and referencing working for Professor Peter Newman.

Faculty of Humanities, Curtin University Sustainability Policy (CUSP) Institute, Building 209, 133 Kent Street, Curtin University Bentley Campus, Perth 6163, Australia

phil.webster@curtin.edu.au

CHINA'S CAPITAL CITY, BEIJING, WHICH functions as the national centre of politics, culture and foreign relations, has risen and fallen with China's economic power and strength. In 2010, China surpassed Japan in terms of nominal gross domestic product (GDP) as the second-largest economy only behind the USA (Barboza, 2010). Beijing has grown in parallel with this economic development and achieved the status of being one of the world's largest cities. The gross regional product (GRP) per capita in Beijing has increased 1,324 times between 1949 and 2012 and is approximately 1.27 times higher than the Chinese average level (Beijing Municipal Bureau of Statistics, 2010). Urban economic growth is usually reflected in the transport systems of any city (Newman and Kenworthy, 1999, 2015). Beijing's transport transitions will be outlined here to show how they reflect the economic agenda of China and its capital city as well as other factors such as the history and politics of the city.

Overview of transport transitions

The data on modal split in Beijing (see Fig. 1) shows the three transitions we will discuss in this paper:

Figure 1 Modal split of Beijing from 1986 to 2012 (excluding walking)

Source: Compiled based on data provided by Beijing Transportation Research Centre (BTRC) (2013)

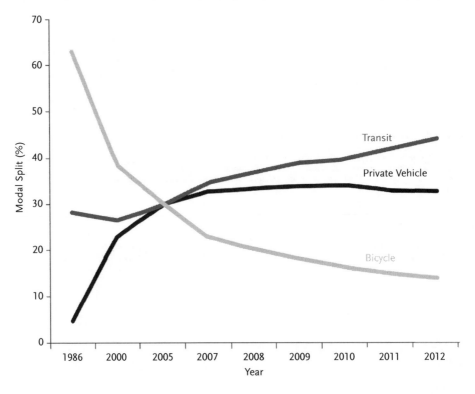

▶ **Phase 1.** The bicycle, the dominant mode from early days until 2001

▶ **Phase 2.** The automobile, the symbol of a modern economy that took over Beijing streets from 2002 to 2010

▶ **Phase 3.** The train, the modern metro that represents the sustainable transport mode of the future and its growth that started in earnest from 2011

The simplest way to understand these transitions is to see how the speed of the modes enabled their rise and fall. Bicycling was faster than walking with its average speed around 15 kph compared to 3–4 kph for walking (Newman and Kenworthy, 1999, 2015). But once cars became available and reasonably affordable, they certainly replaced bikes as their average speed is around 25 kph in most Asian cities (Newman and Kenworthy, 1999, 2015). However, dense Asian cities can slow down very quickly when their streets fill. For example, Bangkok's average traffic speed fell to 13 kph with buses at 9 kph before trains at 35 kph were able to take people at a higher speed. It is our contention that a similar process has occurred in Beijing.

These transitions will be examined in detail to determine their driving forces and to see what the next transition is likely to be in Beijing.

Phase 1: the bicycle (1949–2001)

The ancient city of Beijing developed like all cities around walking and cycling (Newman and Kenworthy, 1999). The dense urban fabric featuring flat terrain and Hutong (small alleys) grew around the ability to walk and cycle to most urban destinations. The traditional employment system (so-called dan wei in Chinese) provided a nearby house as a portion of work-related welfare and thus resulted in walkable and cycling-enabled commuting distances (Zhao et al., 2011). Bicycles were officially imported into China in 1897 as luxury items (Esfehani, 2003), and then foreign-operated bicycle factories were transformed into state-owned plants with the New China established in 1949. The 'Flying Pigeon', which was the first fully nationalised brand of Chinese bicycle, was transformed from one bicycle factory built by the Japanese in 1936. From the 1970s, the bicycle was included as one of the traditional marriage symbols 'Three Rounds and Sound'.[1] The bicycle became more available for transport with mass production (see Fig. 2). Bicycle use was also built into the economy and social life in all Chinese cities. China became well known as the 'Kingdom of the Bicycle' in the 1980s.

---

1 'Three Rounds' means bicycle, watch and sewing machine. The 'Sound' refers to the radio.

Figure 2 Nationwide bicycle production in China (10,000 units) 1958–2013

Source: Compiled based on national data provided by National Bureau of Statistics of China (NBSC) (2014a)

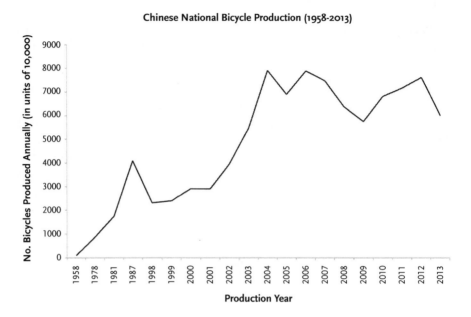

The bicycle fitted into Beijing's walkable urban fabric with ease, enabling the dense, narrow streets to be extended further out. By 1997 there were 9.24 million bicycles for 12.5 million residents in Beijing (Yang *et al.*, 2012). However the end of bicycle transport domination was in sight. Beijing's bicycle mode split in 1986 was 62.7% (probably the highest in any city in the last 50 years) but by 2000 it was down to 38.5% and by 2012 it had dropped to 13.9% (see Fig. 1). The dramatic transition was due to the automobile.

Phase 2: the automobile (2002–2010)

The automobile began to be adopted in China from the early 1990s. Gao *et al.* (2014) suggest that there are four phases in the development of the Chinese automobile industry but the biggest boost came in 2002. The Chinese economy was opened up to the global community in 2001 when China joined the World Trade Organization (WTO), and the Tenth Five-Year Plan (FYP)[2] (2001–2005) encouraged families to purchase private cars. They immediately began developing a world competitive automobile production industry. By 2009 China had

---

2 It refers to a package of incentives to national economy and social development. It has transformed from 'plan' to 'planning' since 2006 according to further transformation of the Chinese macro economy from state-controlled towards market-oriented.

exceeded the USA as the world's largest automobile producer and consumer (Ferrazzi and Goldstein, 2011).

As economic growth accelerated, so did Chinese private automobile ownership (see Fig. 3). From 7.7 million automobiles being privately owned by Chinese in 2001, the number rose to 88.4 million in 2012. This implies an annual growth rate of 24.8%.

Figure 3 Ownership of private vehicles (10,000 units) and growth rate (%)

Source: Compiled based on national data provided by NBSC (2014b)

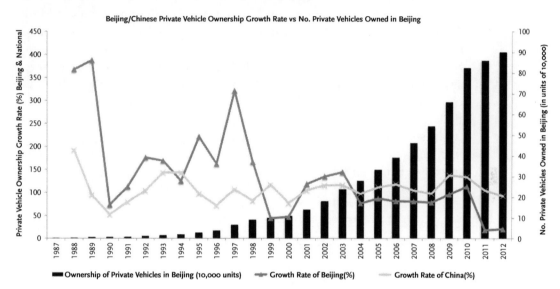

On an individual city basis Beijing has the highest private vehicle ownership per 1000 people in China with 240 as compared to its nearest rivals of Guangzhou (159) and Shanghai (89) in 2012 (GZTPRI, 2012). Beijing's modal share for automobiles dramatically replaced the bicycle in the first decade of the 21st century. Automobiles had just 5% mode share in 1986 (when bikes were at 62.7%) but quickly rose to 34.2% by 2010 while bikes dropped to 16.4%. Supporting this massive modal shift in Beijing was a large increase in road infrastructure investment from US$2.86 billion in 2001 to US$7.59 billion in 2010 (an annual increase of 11.34%). Beijing expressways also experienced a surge in total length during the period (2001–2010) from 335 km to 903 km (representing a growth rate per annum of 11.65%). Finally the number of parking spaces in central Beijing was expanded to 109,000 in 2005, 2.32 times more than was available in 2000 (BTRC, 2001, 2011). These substantial changes in Beijing (and other major Chinese cities) resulted in what is probably one of the most striking social changes in urban history as more and more people left their bikes at home and began travelling by private automobiles.

Economic capacity and Chinese automobile availability were no doubt major factors in this transition but cultural and political encouragement were also influencing factors (see section on 'Underlying processes' below). Private and foreign joint enterprises have gradually replaced the state-owned ones as part of the development of the market economy since 1978 with the 'Reform and Open-up' policy. One of the consequences of the demise of the socialist welfare-oriented housing provision was the collapse of the dan wei system. Hence, the commuting distance accordingly increased, which stimulated the demand for automobiles.

The success of the automobile however was short lived. The automobile did not fit into the dense urban fabric of cities like Beijing. The growth of the automobile hit the wall of traffic congestion and other impacts. The Beijing data show that the automobile modal split has risen, plateaued and then fallen. It has been replaced by metro growth (and its associated other elements of public transport such as integrated buses).

Why did such a rapid transition from bike to car run into such a wall? Most Western cities especially in America and Australia have automobile mode shares of over 80% (Newman and Kenworthy, 1999). There are very obvious reasons why the automobile, the symbol of Western modernism, has not been as dominant in Beijing's transport transition, as in most other cities. The traffic congestion rose very noticeably (see below) to the point where automobile use became far less functional and freeing than advertising would suggest. Average traffic speed was a healthy 45 kph in 1994 but 9 years later it was reduced to 12 kph (Peng, 2004). Associated traffic accidents were very high though this began to improve through better controls and regulations after a few years (see Fig. 4).

Figure 4 Traffic accidents in Beijing from 1996 to 2013

Source: Compiled based on national data provided by NBSC (2013) and BTRC (2001)

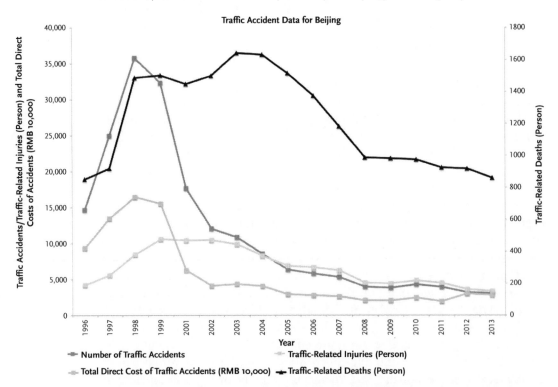

Another problem was that air pollution, as a direct result of private automobile proliferation, grew into a major health issue. Within Chinese cities such as Beijing, primary automobile emissions such as nitrogen oxides (NO_x) and particulate matter (PM) began to supersede primary industry emissions such as sulphur dioxide (SO_2) as the greatest source of urban pollution (Hao and Wang, 2005). The annual average concentration of PM2.5 in Beijing deteriorated to 89.5 ug/m³ in 2013, 2.56 times worse than the national standard (Beijing Municipal Environmental Protection Bureau/BMEPB, 2013) and 8.95 times inferior to World Health Organization (WHO) guidelines (2005). The contribution of vehicles to the PM2.5 was calculated as high as 31% in Beijing (BMEPB, 2014).

This required action, as it was a negative reflection on the nation's capital. In addition the strengthening global agenda to make major commitments to cut fossil fuel consumption ensured that doing nothing to curtail automobile growth was no longer a viable option.

In reality, the sheer functionality of Beijing was never greatly assisted by the automobile. After millennia of developing a culture around dense living with narrow streets that are suited to pedestrians and cyclists, the automobile just did not fit. Beijing literally hit the wall of its urban fabric. A similar process has begun in most developed cities where motor vehicles can no longer fit into the fabric of the city. This global phenomenon of 'peak car', is based on the value of economic productivity associated with dense urbanism in old cities, which is increasingly being recognised for its benefits in overcoming automobile dependence (Newman and Kenworthy, 2011, 2015). Beijing is possibly one of the first emerging cities to begin demonstrating that a better, more sustainable transport system is needed for economic productivity as well as environmental and social/health goals, as shown below.

Phase 3: the train (2011–)

Growth in private automobile ownership and massive expansions in automobile production capacity have labelled China as the new 'Giant' of the automobile industry since 2009 (Gao et al., 2014). A similar transport transition also emerged around 2008—a significant increase in rail infrastructure development within major Chinese cities such as Beijing (see Table 1). The transition then developed from 2011 affected by a package of transportation demand management in Beijing, including the termination of national pro-car policies designed to overcome the 2008 global financial crisis, incentives to train use through new infrastructure and restrictions on private car ownership and use. A large part of the reason behind this was the negative impacts associated with massive automobile proliferation within Chinese urban centres that were traditionally built around walking, cycling and other non-motorised modes of transport, while being poorly suited to large volumes of automobile traffic. The average speed of traffic in central Beijing decreased from 45 kph in 1994 to 12 kph in 2003, which is as low as any other congested city in the world despite much lower automobile ownership levels (Peng, 2004). More recent data is less certain though Guilford (2014) suggests that in 2014–5 the average speed remains fairly unchanged from 2003 speeds. The Beijing Government does not believe that average traffic speeds will exceed 15 kph in 2015 (Beijing International, 2015). Such speeds greatly reduce the allure of the private automobile and encourage urban transport planners to look for alternative solutions.

This negative reaction to the automobile began to be seen officially with controls on vehicle overuse that built on interventions for the 2008 Olympic Games hosted by Beijing through road space rationing from 1 July to 20 September 2008 (BTMB, 2008). In December 2010 the government announced their further effort to cap total private vehicle ownership (BMCT, 2010). Unlike the Singapore-style paid auction system implemented in Shanghai, Beijing adopted the unpaid lottery to distribute new licence plates to public applicants. The quotas on new car registration have been further tightened from 240,000 in 2011 to 150,000 in 2014, which aims to cap total vehicle ownership at less than 6 million by 2017 (Beijing Municipal Government 2013). By 2011 the private ownership growth rate in Beijing had dropped to 4.25% compared to 23.37% in the rest of China (after being 25.27% in Beijing in 2010; see Fig. 3).

However, the biggest impact on automobile use growth has been the dramatic increase in the use of the Beijing Metro. Beijing's municipal government initially put forward its subway construction plans in 1953 for military defence on the basis of technological assistance from the former Soviet Union and East Germany (Gao, n.d.). The first line of Chinese urban rail transport in Beijing did not trial run until 1969 due to the Sino-Soviet split in 1960 and the Great Chinese Famine of 1959–1961 (Strickfaden and Devlieger, 2011). However, the 2008 Olympics led to the rapid building of the Beijing Metro system (see Table 1). Its success has bred continued growth. It grew from 2 lines, 54 km of track and around 400 million passengers a year in 2001 to 22 lines, 527 km of track and around 3,387 million passengers a year in 2014 (around 9 million passengers a day). This makes it one of the most successful rail systems in the world and certainly one of the fastest growing (Newman et al., 2013). The mode share of metro increased from 3.6% to 13.8% between 2000 and 2011 while the bus share grew slowly from 22.9% to 28.2% over the same period. Thus we have chosen 2010 as the key date for the transformation of Beijing to a third priority in its transport system.

Table 1 Development of Beijing Subway (2001–2014)

Source: Compiled based on data provided by BTRC (2013), CRT (2014) and Beijing Infrastructure Investment Company LTD (2014)

Year	Number of operational lines	Operational length (km)	Annual patronage (100 million)
2001	2	54	4.42
2002	3	75	4.82
2003	4	114	4.72
2004	4	114	6.07
2005	4	114	6.8

Continued

2006	4	114	7.03
2007	5	142	6.55
2008	8	200	12.2
2009	9	228	14.2
2010	14	336	18.46
2011	15	372	21.93
2012	16	442	24.6
2013	18	465	32.05
2014	22	527	33.87

Economic growth has continued in Beijing during the 21st century but now the city is directing this (in transport terms), into trains rather than automobiles. Throughout the past 20 years of urban growth in China and in Beijing the cities have continued to build densely in the same way that most other Asian nations have built. The 10–20 storey high buildings of Beijing may have gone further out than the ancient walking city has grown, but the corridors of development were ideally formed as transit urban fabric that would easily absorb an electric rail system with fast connections across the city. Thus the historic Beijing urban fabric could be retained and enabled to grow without the kind of automobile-based problems of the previous automobile transition phase. The metro was thus an enabler of sustainable transport and sustainable urban development (Newman and Kenworthy, 1999, 2015).

Underlying processes guiding the transitions

Three processes are suggested to be critical to the three transport transitions in Beijing (and probably all Chinese cities):

▶ Administrative guidance

▶ Urban fabric

▶ Economic development

Administrative guidance

China has drawn up Five-Year Plans to guide its cities and regions towards further economic and social development. In Table 2 the past seven Five-Year Plans are summarised in terms of their core transport outcomes. Each of the transitions from bike to automobile and from automobile to train, have been deliberately planned. Chinese automotive industry is still regarded as a significant sector; however, there is an explicit move towards the development of new energy vehicles (NEVs) and prioritising public transport, especially the metro.

Table 2 Evolution of China's consecutive FYPs on private vehicles and public transport

Source: Compiled based on data provided by People's Congress of People's Republic of China (1981, 1986, 1991, 1996, 2001, 2006, 2011)

Sixth FYP (1981–1985)	The first FYP since 1978 was themed as adjustment of the existing freight vehicle production
Seventh FYP (1986–1990)	It was proposed that the auto sector should be regarded as a pillar industry of the national economy to meet transportation demand
Eighth FYP (1991–1995)	The role of the auto sector in the national economy was determined to be more than satisfying the transportation industry The development priority was shifted from freight vehicles to passenger automobiles
Ninth FYP (1996–2000)	It was determined that the auto industry, which performs as an engine of economic growth, needs to achieve mass production Furthermore it was made clear that a self-owned technology system for the automobile industry that has been running under joint venture should be built for gaining access to the WTO
Tenth FYP (2001–2005)	It officially proposed the concept 'Encouraging Passenger Cars into Family' It aimed to energetically foster public transport including rail transit in megacities at the same time It proposed a sustainable development strategy and other measures to alleviate global climate change but without detail on how
Eleventh FYP (2006–2010)	'Prioritising Transportation industry' was listed as an economic priority The development of energy-saving and environmentally friendly vehicles was encouraged as a means to control GHG emissions. Strengthening vehicle fuel economy standards was seen as another key priority aimed to assist with the development of a circular economy Rail transport was identified as a key priority in both Chinese qualified megacities and significant urban agglomerations
Twelfth FYP (2011–2015)	NEVs were identified, as one of China's strategic emerging industries (SEI) Specific sections of the plan such as those entitled 'Establishing Integrated Transportation Systems (ITS)', and 'Prioritising Public Transport', serve to stress the importance of further development of public transport including rail The Chapter 'Actively Respond to Global Climate Change' suggests that traffic-related GHG emissions should be controlled

Urban fabric

There is an inherent logic to shifting to automobiles if only an economic consideration is provided but every city has its own combination of walking city fabric, transit city fabric and automobile city fabric (Newman and Kenworthy, 2015). Beijing and other Chinese cities use mostly walking and transit fabric and are thus always going to struggle fitting in automobiles. As discussed above the new transit fabric of the metro is enabling the traditional dense corridors of Beijing to be better served than by the congested traffic of the second transport transition.

Economic development

National economic growth increasingly depends on urban economic growth (Glaeser, 2011; Florida, 2010). In Phase 1 the bicycle-based city needed modernising, but by the end of Phase 2 it was clear that economic growth in Beijing could not work without a more green or sustainable transport foundation. In recent times this transition is being called the 'Green Economy', or 'Green Growth', (UNEP, 2011; OECD, 2011). The result is that GDP is becoming decoupled from fossil fuels (UNEP, 2011; Newman and Kenworthy, 2015).

In Figure 5 it is clear that China is decoupling its GDP from oil consumption. At least part of the reason behind this is the rapid growth of electric trains like that in Beijing's Metro, which is now able to out-compete car use because average traffic speeds are low (Peng, 2004; Guilford, 2014; Beijing International, 2015).

Figure 5 China GDP vs. oil consumption

Source: Compiled based on data provided by NBSC (2013)

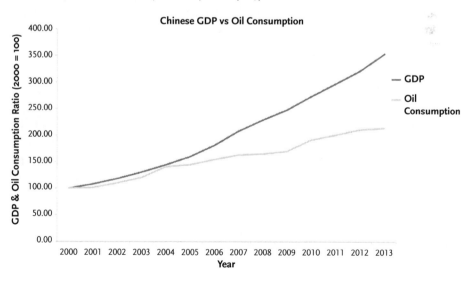

There were in fact 95 metros being built or operating in Chinese cities by the end of 2014 (see Fig. 6) and each step in the growth of patronage means that less oil is driving the economy.

As well as urban electric public transport growth there has also been dramatic growth in high-speed electric rail between Chinese cities (over 11,132 km was in operation by September 2014) (International Union of Railways/UIC). Oil will also be reduced by the development of electric private vehicles and on Chinese streets there are now over 250 million electric vehicles (mostly E-bikes and E-Scooters) (Newman, 2014). The growth of these electric scooters and bikes depends on the travel distances being reasonably short; over half of the daily trips by Beijing residents were within 5 km in 2012 (BTRC, 2013).

Figure 6 Total expected length of metro construction by end of 2015

Source: Compiled based on data provided by Lohry *et al.* (2014)

The next transition phase?

Based on the evidence presented and the analysis provided there is likely to be a continuing growth of Phase 3—the train. The fundamental urban fabric of Chinese cities like Beijing, the political culture and the economic growth context, all suggest more focus on non-automobile-based economic development.

Electric bikes and electric trains are likely to be the basis of future sustainable transport trends in China, especially as the world begins to compete around the rapidity of their transition away from carbon intensive activity. Figure 7 shows the potential projection to 2030 in Beijing based on a continuation of recent trends.

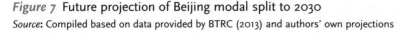
Figure 7 Future projection of Beijing modal split to 2030

Source: Compiled based on data provided by BTRC (2013) and authors' own projections

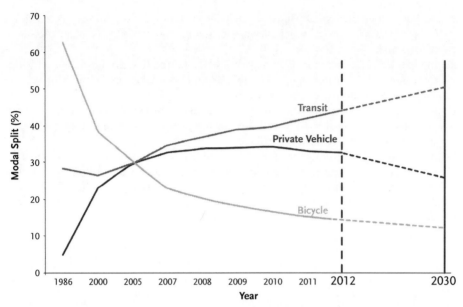

Perhaps a more dramatic direction change will be the need to better manage the traffic that is left with a greater emphasis on walkable urban design characteristics (Gehl, 2010). The six most walkable cities in the US have 38% higher GDP than the rest (Leinberger and Lynch, 2014). Such focus is likely to mean even more careful treatment of the Chinese urban fabric to ensure that sustainable mobility and economic growth can be achieved together.

Conclusions

The three transition phases of Beijing based on bikes, automobiles and trains, are related to the economic and political drivers in the city but these are expressed in the fundamental urban fabric of the traditional dense urbanism of Chinese history and culture. The next phase is therefore likely to see these factors continue to create less automobile-dependent and more sustainable transport-oriented cities, especially in Beijing.

References

Barboza, D. (2010), 'China passes Japan as second-largest economy,' The New York Times (16th August), Available at: http://www.nytimes.com/2010/08/16/business/global/16yuan.html?pagewanted=all&_r=0s [Accessed 11/01/2015].

Beijing Infrastructure Investment Company Ltd. (2014), 'Average Working Day Patronage in Beijing Metro 2014,' Available at http://www.bii.com.cn/705-2063-5114.aspx [Accessed 14/03/2015].

Beijing International. (2015), 'Driving speed in Beijing may be only 15 km in 2015,' Available at http://www.ebeijing.gov.cn/BeijingInformation/BeijingNewsUpdate/t1128512.htm [Accessed 10/03/2015].

Beijing Municipal Commission of Transport (BMCT). (2010), 'Interim Provisions on Vehicles Quantity Control in Beijing,' Available at http://www.bjjtgl.gov.cn/publish/portal0/tab63/info21956.htm [Accessed 11/01/2015].

Beijing Municipal Environmental Protection Bureau (BMEPB). (2013), 'Beijing Environment Statement' Available at http://www.bjepb.gov.cn/bjepb/323474/ 331443/331937/333896/ 395964/index.html [Accessed 14/03/2015].

Beijing Municipal Environmental Protection Bureau (BMEPB). (2014), 'What are the Prime Culprits leading to the Haze: vehicle is the biggest contributor in Beijing' Available at http://finance.people.com.cn/n/2014/0426/c1004-24945251.html [Accessed 15/03/2015].

Beijing Municipal Government (BMG). (2013), 'Clean Air Action Plan 2013-2017,' Available at http://zhengwu.beijing.gov.cn/ghxx/qtgh/t1324558.htm [Accessed 23/11/2014].

Beijing Traffic Management Bureau (BTMB). (2008), 'Announcement on Temporary Traffic Management Measures for Motor Vehicles in Beijing During the Olympics and Paralympics Games,' Available at http://zhengwu.beijing.gov.cn/gzdt/gggs/t975714.htm [Accessed 11/01/2015].

Beijing Transportation Research Centre (BTRC). (2001), 'Beijing Transport Development,' (Annual Report), BTRC, Beijing, CHI.

Beijing Transportation Research Centre (BTRC). (2011), 'Beijing Transport Development,' (Annual Report), BTRC, Beijing, CHI

Beijing Transportation Research Centre (BTRC). (2013), 'Beijing Transport Development,' (Annual Report), BTRC, Beijing, CHI.

China Rail Transit (CRT). (2014), 'China Urban Rail Transit Operation Length and Stations by the end of 2013,' Available at http://www.rail-transit.com/Detail_News.aspx?id=22696 [Accessed 11/01/2015].

China.org.cn. (n.d.), 'Summary of the 6th Five Year Plan (1981–1985),' Available at http://www.china.org.cn/english/MATERIAL/157619.htm [Accessed 11/01/2015].

China.org.cn. (n.d.), 'Summary of the 7th Five Year Plan (1986–1990),' Available at http://www.china.org.cn/english/MATERIAL/157620.htm [Accessed 11/01/2015].

China.org.cn. (n.d.), 'Summary of the 8th Five Year Plan (1991–1995),' Available at http://www.china.org.cn/english/MATERIAL/157625.htm [Accessed 11/01/2015].

China.org.cn. (n.d.), 'Summary of the 9th Five Year Plan (1996–2000),' Available at http://www.china.org.cn/english/MATERIAL/157627.htm [Accessed 11/01/2015].

China.org.cn. (n.d.), 'Summary of the 10th Five Year Plan (2001–2005),' Available at http://www.china.org.cn/english/features/38198.htm [Accessed 11/01/2015].

China.org.cn. (n.d.), 'Summary of the 11th Five Year Plan (2006–2010),' Available at http://www.china.org.cn/english/features/guideline/156529.htm [Accessed 11/01/2015].

Esfehani, A.M. (2003), 'The Bicycle's Long Way to China: The Appropriation of Cycling as a Foreign Cultural Technique 1860–1940,' (Paper presented at the 14th International Cycling History Conference), 25–28 February, San Francisco, USA.

Ferrazzi, M., & Goldstein, A. (2011), 'The New Geography of Automotive Manufacturing,' (Briefing Paper), Chatham House, London, UK.

Florida, R. (2010), 'The Great Reset: How New Ways of Living and Working Drive Post-Crash Prosperity,' Harper Collins, New York, USA.

Gao, J.L. (n.d.), 'The detailed information on the first line of subway construction in China,' Available at http://cpc.people.com.cn/GB/85037/85039/7541412.html [Accessed 11/01/2015].

Gao, Y., Kenworthy, J. & Newman, P. (2014), 'Growth of a Giant: A Historical and Current Perspective on the Chinese Automobile Industry,' (Paper presented at the 42nd European Transport Conference), 29 September – 1 October, Association for European Transport, Frankfurt, GER.

Gehl, J. (2010), 'Cities for people,' Island Press, Washington DC, USA.

Glaeser, E. (2011), 'The Triumph of the City, How our Greatest Invention makes us Richer, Smarter, Greener, Healthier and Happier,' Penguin Press, London, UK.

Guangzhou Transport Planning Research Institute (GZTPRI). (2012), 'Guangzhou Transport Development,' (Annual Report), Available at http://www. gztpri.com/upload/nianbao/annual_report_2012.pdf [Accessed 11/01/2015].

Guilford, G. (2014), 'A big reason Beijing is Polluted: The Average Car goes 7.5 Miles per Hour,' Available at http://qz.com/163178/a-big-reason-beijing-is-polluted-the-average-car-goes-7-5-miles-per-hour/ [Accessed 10/03/2015].

Hao, J., & Wang, L. (2005), 'Improving urban air quality in China: Beijing case study,' Journal of the Air & Waste Management Association, 55(9), 1298-1305.

International Union of Railways (UIC). (2014), 'High Speed Lines in the World,' Available at http://www.uic.org/IMG/pdf/20140901_high_speed_lines_in_the_world.pdf [Accessed 15/03/2015].

Leinberger, C., & Lynch, P. (2014), 'Foot Traffic Ahead, Ranking Walking Urbanism in America's largest Metros,' (Research Report), Centre for Real Estate and Urban Analysis, School of Business, Washington University, Washington DC, USA.

Lohry, G., Yiu, A. Yuanyuan, T. & Yue, L. (2014), 'Urban Mobility China,' Available at http://www.urbanmobilitychina.com/tag/metro/ [Accessed 11/01/2015].

National Bureau of Statistics of China (NBSC). (2013), 'Annual Yearbook,' Available at http://www.stats.gov.cn/tjsj/ndsj/2013/indexeh.htm [Accessed 11/01/ 2015].

National Bureau of Statistics of China (NBSC). (2014a), 'National Data: National Production of Bicycles (1958–2013)' Available at http://data.stats.gov.cn/search/keywordlist2?keyword= 自行车产量 [Accessed 20/12/2014].

National Bureau of Statistics of China (NBSC). (2014b), 'National Data: Ownership of Private Vehicles in Beijing (1987–2012),' Available at http://data.stats.gov.cn/workspace/index?a=q&type=global&dbcode=fsnd&m=fsnd&dimension=zb&code=A0G0801&region=110000&time=2012,2012 [Accessed 11/01 2015].

Newman, P. (2014), 'Sustainability: Are We Winning?' Available at https://www.youtube.com/watch?v=6RFiyM89rbk [Accessed 27/01/2015].

Newman, p., & Kenworthy, J. (1999), 'Sustainability and Cities: Overcoming Automobile Dependence,' Island Press, Washington DC, USA.

Newman, P., & Kenworthy, J. (2011), 'Peak Car Use: Understanding the Demise of Automobile Dependence,' World Transport Policy and Practice, 17(2), 32-42.

Newman, P., & Kenworthy, J. (2015), 'The End of Automobile Dependence,' Island Press, Washington DC, USA.

Newman, P., Kenworthy, J. & Glazebrook, G. (2013), 'Peak Car and the Rise of Global Rail: Why this is happening and what it means for large and small cities,' Journal of Transportation Technologies, 3(4), 272-87.

Organisation for Economic Co-Operation and Development (OECD). (2011), 'Towards Green Growth,' (Strategic Report), OECD, Paris, FRA.

Peng, Z.-R. (2004), 'Urban Transportation Strategies in Chinese Cities and their Impacts on the Urban Poor,' (Report), Center for Advanced Spatial Information Research, University of Wisconsin-Milwaukee, Milwaukee, USA.

People's Congress of the People's Republic of China (PCPRC). (2011), 'Twelfth Five Year Plan (2011–2015),' Available at http://www.china.com.cn/policy/txt/2011-03/16/content_22156007.htm [Accessed 11/01/2015].

Strickfaden, M., & Devlieger, P. (2011), 'Empathy through Accumulating Techné: Designing an Accessible Metro,' The Design Journal, 14(2), 207-29.

United Nations Environment Programme (UNEP), (2011), 'Decoupling Natural Resource Use and Environmental impacts from Economic Growth,' UNEP, Geneva, SWI.

World Health Organisation (WHO). (2005), 'WHO Air quality guidelines for particulate matter, ozone, nitrogen dioxide and sulfur dioxide,' Available at http://whqlibdoc.who.int/hq/2006/WHO_SDE_PHE_OEH_06.02_eng.pdf [Accessed 14/03/2015].

Yang, M., Wang, Q. Zhao, J. & Zacharias, J. (2014), 'The Rise and Decline of the Bicycle in Beijing,' Transport Review: Submitted.

Zhao, Z., and Larson, K. (2011), 'Special Assessments as a Value Capture Strategy for Public Transit Finance,' Public Works Management Policy, 16(4), 320-40.a

DOI: [10.9774/GLEAF.8757.2014.ju.00004]

Evaluating Market Competitiveness of Battery Electric Cars in the Chinese Market[*]

Jiuyu Du and Minggao Ouyang
Tsinghua University, China

Jingfu Chen
Tsinghua University and Harbin University of Science and Technology, China

Mingming Gao
Harbin University of Science and Technology, China

To promote the penetration of new energy vehicles, the Ministry of Science and Technology of the People's Republic of China (MOST) launched the 'National Science and Technology Infrastructure Program', under which the new energy vehicles database was established. The electric vehicles market competitiveness evaluation system is developed based on the database. The evaluation system can provide the theoretical basis for automotive manufacturers to design and produce vehicles, and for the government to develop policy instruments. Furthermore, the market competitiveness of electric vehicles can be improved. First, we chose reasonable indexes for evaluating electric vehicles based on the database and Chinese consumer survey results. Then, each index was quantified by referring to the elastic search method of function score. The analytic hierarchy process (AHP) was applied to determine the weights of all indexes in the system. Finally, competitiveness predictions of electric vehicles were calculated with the vehicle dynamic and economic models. The results show that class B electric cars are more competitive in the current electric vehicle market. With the development of electric vehicle technologies, A class electric cars will gradually exceed class B. Class Aoo electric cars also have strong competitiveness in the Chinese market, which can be attributable to their cheaper prices.

● Electric vehicles

● New energy vehicles database

● Market competitiveness

● Analytic hierarchy process

* This research is funded by MOST (Ministry of Science and Technology) 'International S&T Cooperation Program of China' under contract No. 2014DFG71590 and 2012DFA81190, and National Science and Technology Infrastructure Program under contract No. 2013BAG06B04.

Dr **Jiuyu Du** is an assistant professor at Tsinghua University. She focuses on advanced vehicle powertrain design, simulation, energy-saving and new energy vehicle system analysis, performance analysis and evaluation of vehicle powertrain, and electric vehicle R&D technology roadmap.

State Key Laboratory of Automotive Safety and Energy, Room 311, Tsinghua University, Beijing 100084, China

dujiuyu@tsinghua.edu.cn

Jingfu Chen is a graduate student in the Department of Automation, Harbin University of Science and Technology. He is a member of the US–China Clean Vehicle Consortium. His current focuses are plug-in electric vehicles and electric vehicle R&D technology roadmap.

State Key Laboratory of Automotive Safety and Energy, Room 311, Tsinghua University, Beijing 100084, China

chenjingfu@tsinghua.edu.cn

Mingming Gao received his BS degree in electrical engineering from the Harbin University of Science and Technology, Harbin, China, in 2014. He is currently a Master's postgraduate in Power Electronics and Power Drive, Harbin University of Science and Technology. His research interest is the powertrain control of electric vehicles.

College of Electrical and Electronics Engineering, Room G0718, Harbin University of Science and Technology, Harbin 150080, China

m851767610@126.com

Professor **Ouyang Minggao** is the Director of the State Key Laboratory of Energy and Safety and Director of the US–China Clean Vehicle Consortium. His main research and teaching work includes: system and control of internal combustion engine, hybrid powertrain system and control, and vehicular powertrain system analysis and strategy planning.

State Key Laboratory of Automotive Safety and Energy, Room 311, Tsinghua University, Beijing 100084, China

ouymg@tsinghua.edu.cn

THE TRANSPORT SECTOR, AS A major oil consumer and greenhouse gas emitter, accounted for 26% of the world's energy use and 23% of the energy-related greenhouse gas emissions (GHG) in 2004 [1]. Road transportation is responsible for over 90% of these emissions [2] [3]. To overcome the resulting air pollution and energy security issues, governments are encouraging automobile manufacturers to develop electric vehicles (EVs) and hybrid electric vehicles (HEVs) [4]. With the EV development, many different EV brands with different prices and performances were introduced into the market. Consumers' purchase decisions are mostly determined by the competitiveness of these vehicle products. The EV market is different in each country, and consumers have different preferences.

According to statistics, the automobile industry in developed countries is expanding the EV market, such as in the US, Japan and Europe. The EV market shares of five countries are over 1%. The US was the best performing country in 2014, with more than 100,000 annual sales. China's EV market is in the rapid growth period, second in the world in terms of cumulative sales. EV sales almost doubled in 2013. The highest monthly sale of BAIC EV150 was over 1,700, which created the EV sale record in a single month. Mini electric cars regards leasehold as the main promotion method. Its sales were about 17,000 in 2014. As can be seen from these data, the Chinese EV market is taking off. Under the current favourable policies [5–7], the technology roadmap is burgeoning for China.

Under the current and future market, industry and technology conditions, the state and enterprises are increasingly concerned about what kinds of cars are more competitive. In the present research, established mathematical models are applied to solve this problem, such as MA3T [8]. These methods are suitable for the incubation period of the market, because the results can be deduced without big data. However, in the formative period, the theory with big real data would be more suitable for the real market. No prior research has used a similar method to ours. Therefore, the Ministry of Science and Technology (MOST) set up the 'National Science and Technology Infrastructure Program' to establish the new energy vehicles database, which can be used to support rational EV development and to design the Chinese EV technology roadmap. On the basis of the database, this paper conducts classification analysis on EVs on the Chinese market. The most competitive car class is found through the EVs market competitiveness evaluation system.

Methods

Database overview

The new energy vehicles database covers EVs in the Chinese market and model vehicles which are developed by Chinese automobile enterprises. As market competitiveness is the main research object, EVs in the Chinese market are selected for analysis. The database includes basic information, vehicle perform-ance, sales, costs, facilities, and the main parameters of key components such as battery and motor, adding up to a total of more than 70 cross-entries.

Electric vehicle class

Vehicles have a variety of classifications. According to the wheelbase, EVs in the database are divided into mini-cars (Aoo class), small cars (Ao class), com-pact cars (A class), midsize cars (B class), medium and large cars (C class) and luxury cars (D class). The Aoo class wheelbase is between 2 m and 2.2 m, such as Chery QQ3 EV. The Ao class wheelbase is between 2.3 m and 2.45 m. The BAIC E150 EV is a typical Ao class car. The wheelbase of the A class ranges between approximately 2.45 m and 2.65 m, accounting for 30.5% of the total. The C class and D class have impressive appearance and their wheelbases are over 2.8 m. However, these classes are rare in the database.

Figure 1 Class distribution in vehicle database

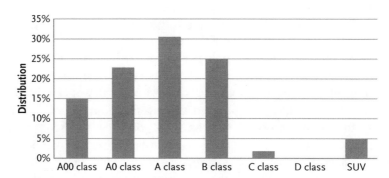

In terms of the vehicle classes, compact cars (A class) occupy the highest share. Mini-cars (Aoo class), small cars (Ao class) and midsize cars (B class) also account for a sizeable share. About 5% of the remaining vehicles belong to the SUV class. In the present market status, the above-mentioned EVs are studied in this paper.

Dynamic performance

Top speed is one important measure of vehicle dynamic performance and is a concern for most consumers.

Figure 2 Top speed distribution of cars in database

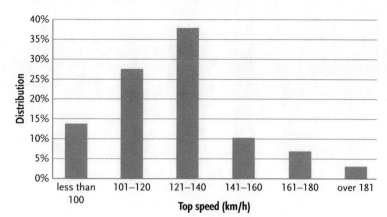

As shown in Figure 2, the top speeds of most vehicles are in the range of 100–140 km/h, which accounts for 60% of the total.

Acceleration is also an important reference index for consumers and a key factor influencing the market competitiveness of vehicles.

Figure 3 Acceleration time (0–100 km/h) distribution of EVs in database

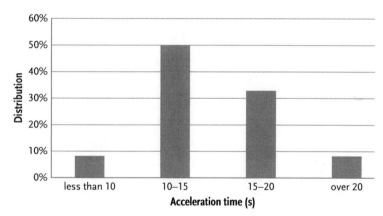

According to the acceleration distribution of various vehicles, more than 80% of vehicle acceleration times in the database are distributed within 10 s to 20 s.

Energy efficiency

Operating costs of vehicles are mainly determined by the fuel economy. A small change in electricity consumption per hundred kilometres can impact greatly on the whole life cycle cost. According to the database, electricity consumption per hundred kilometres are concentrated between 10 kWh and 20 kWh, as shown in Figure 4.

Figure 4 Electricity consumption ratio in database

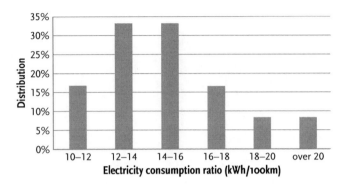

As can be seen from the statistical results, the power consumption of most vehicles is around 14 kWh/100 km.

Industrialisation status

The vehicle price determines the consumer groups. In the EV market competitiveness evaluation system, price plays a crucial role. Considering the vehicles are mainly distributed from the Aoo class to B class, this paper focuses on the vehicles priced under 250,000 Yuan.

Figure 5 Car prices distribution in database

The vehicles in the database have a wide price distribution covering the needs of most consumers; 50% of vehicle prices are around 200,000 Yuan. Prices below 100,000 Yuan also account for a considerable part of the market.

Habits of users

Due to the longer charging time and inadequate charging infrastructure, driving range has a significant impact on consumer travel habits [9]. The vehicle kilometres travelled daily (VKT) is a unique problem of EVs and a strong concern for consumers.

Figure 6 Driving range distribution of cars in database

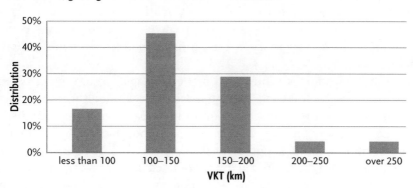

As the statistics indicate, more than 80% of driving ranges in the database are from 100 km to 200 km. VKT of less than 100 km are attributed to the A00 class mostly, because a shorter driving range still can meet the special demands of A00 class consumers.

Method of market competitiveness evaluation

For evaluation of the competitiveness of products, all direct or indirect effects of competitive factors should be fully taken into account. Any situation that requires structuring, measurement and/or synthesis is a good candidate for application of the analytic hierarchy process (AHP). For example, the Canadian British Columbia Ferry Corporation used the AHP in the selection of products, suppliers and consultants. When using a decision tree to analyse alternative choices, the AHP is used to derive probabilities for the choice nodes of the decision tree, as well as to derive priorities for alternatives at the extremities of the decision tree [10]. From the decision-making perspective, the new energy vehicles database can be seen as a decision tree. Vehicle market competitiveness is the decision-making objective that should be evaluated by structuring, measurement and synthesis of the renewable vehicles database. Therefore, APH is a reasonable way to analyse vehicle market competitiveness.

Vehicle market competitiveness evaluation indexes are established by referring to consumer requirements and following several principles of the operability, comparability, importance and industry features. Then, the scientific method is selected to quantify the evaluation index. The different importance levels of each indicator in the EV market evaluation system are determined, which means that each indicator is given corresponding weight. The function score method of elastic search combined with the Gauss function [11] is applied to quantify the evaluation index. AHP [12] is used to determine weights. Finally, product competitiveness results and predictions of electric vehicles could be calculated with the vehicle dynamic and economic models [13] [14].

Evaluation index

Referring to a large number of Chinese EV market research reports, the key factors for Chinese consumers in turn are dynamic performance, economy and comfort. These factors are set as primary indicators for the evaluation system.

From the viewpoint of achieving a higher average speed, vehicle dynamic performance can be evaluated through three aspects: 1) top speed; 2) acceleration time (0–100 km/h); and 3) maximum climbable gradient. Cars usually run on good surfaces and have higher top speed and shorter acceleration time, so the maximum climbable gradient does not need to be stressed generally [15]. This paper also considers the impact of rated battery power, battery capacity, battery weight, motor rated power, motor weight, the driving range and vehicle mass as the relative indexes, which can influence the vehicle dynamic performance.

The survey results show that 80% of consumers have a higher sensitivity to fuel economy in the Chinese EV market. We classified the cost to the consumer in terms of vehicle purchase cost, fuel cost, non-fuel operation and maintenance (O&M) cost, and alternative transportation cost [16]. It should be noted that the vehicle's residual value is not included in our consumer cost analysis; this value should be subtracted from the total cost if considered. In the new energy vehicles database, vehicle purchase cost and fuel cost correspond to the vehicle price and fuel economy (electricity), respectively. The disadvantages of EV batteries include the high cost and capacity degradation [17]. Therefore, the price of battery capacity ratio (Yuan/kWh) is applied to represent the non-fuel O&M cost. We ignored vehicle residual value and alternative transportation cost mainly because of a lack of data, especially regarding the residual value of battery EVs. It will be studied in the future.

Automotive performance requirements are not only power and economy, but also seeking to improve driving comfort. Automobile comfort is mainly based on passenger experience. It is not only related to the vibration characteristics of the vehicle structure, but is also affected by the environment and the passenger's physiological and psychological condition. This paper only uses car space and driving behaviour to evaluate automobile comfort because of the limited data in the database. The evaluation indexes include vehicle size, number of seats, driving range and charging time (slow charge). The number of seats and the vehicle size indicate the comfort of the vehicle's interior space. Range anxiety and long charging time are the current shortcomings of EVs, which influence consumer habits. Therefore, they are closely related to vehicle comfort. EV market competitiveness evaluation indexes at all levels are shown in Table 1.

Table 1 EV market competitiveness evaluation indexes

Level 1	Level 2	Level 3
Dynamic performance	Performance	Top speed
		Acceleration time (0–100 km/h)
		Driving range
	Parameters	Vehicle mass
	Battery system	Battery rated power
		Battery capacity
		Pack mass
	Motor drive system	Motor rated power
Energy efficiency	Parameters	Vehicle price
		Fuel economy (electricity)
	Battery system	price of battery capacity ratio (Yuan/kWh)
	Motor drive system	price of motor power ratio (Yuan/kW)
	Others	Electricity price
Comfort	Parameters	Vehicle size
		Number of seats
		Charging time (slow charge)
	Others	Driving range

Quantification and evaluation of indexes

Elastic search is a tool for cloud computing, which has a strong ability to display data. Function score is a key function in the elastic search, which can present and evaluate results in the form of scores. Considering the features of the index data in the database and system requirements, the Gauss decay function is applied to evaluate these indexes. Decay functions score a document with a function that decays depending on the distance of a numeric field value of the document from a user given origin. The Gauss decay function has a higher smoothness. To use distance scoring on a query that has numerical fields, the user has to define an origin and a scale for each field. The origin is needed to define the 'central point' from which the distance is calculated, and the scale to define the rate of decay. Then the decay could be calculated. The final evaluation function is shown as follows:

$$S(doc) = \exp\left(-\frac{(fieldvalue_{doc} - origin)^2}{2\sigma^2}\right) \tag{1}$$

where, $fieldvalue_{doc}$ is the index data from the database and σ ensures the scores are in a reasonable range.

$$\sigma^2 = -scale^2 \big/ (2 \cdot \log(decay)) \tag{2}$$

Index weight determination

The rationality of the index weight assignment is significant to the scientific rationality of the evaluation results. To guarantee a scientific and effective evaluation system, the weight of each indicator of assignment must be scientific and objective. Considering the obvious hierarchy of the market competitiveness evaluation index in electric vehicles, this paper values each of the indexes with the level analysis method. The level analysis method puts the problem into several factors then divides them into a certain hierarchy; then expert system responses the importance between elements a_i and a_j in criterion A [18]. To quantify the judgment matrix, it generally refers to Saaty's 1~9 proportion criteria method based on the analysis of mental habit and psychics research results, this method is accepted by users and is shown in Table 2.

Table 2 1~9 quantitative criteria

Criteria	Implication
1	For A_m, a_i and a_j are equally significant
3	For A_m, a_i is slightly more significant than a_j
5	For A_m, a_i is obviously more significant than a_j
7	For A_m, a_i is much more significant than a_j
9	For A_m, a_i is absolutely more significant than a_j
2, 4, 6, 8	Between two quantitative criteria

where i is the matrix row, j is the matrix column

The main steps are described as follows:

First, set A as objective, a_i, a_j (i, j=1,2,3,...,n) is the element, r_{ij} is the importance of a_i to a_j, and the judgement matrix A is formed.

$$A = \begin{matrix} r_{11} & r_{12} & \cdots & r_{1n} \\ r_{21} & r_{22} & \cdots & r_{2n} \\ \vdots & \vdots & \ddots & \vdots \\ r_{a1} & r_{a2} & \cdots & r_{an} \end{matrix} \tag{3}$$

Then, find the maximum characteristic root λ_{max} with its eigenvector ω, and the importance of each evaluation factor (index weight) is obtained by normalisation processing ω.

The Journal of Sustainable Mobility Volume 2 Issue 1 *June 2015* © Greenleaf Publishing 2015

$$A\omega = \lambda_{max}\omega \tag{4}$$

Finally, check the consistency of A. The purpose is to verify the rationality of the index weight; the checking formulas are expressed as follows:

$$CR = CI/RI \tag{5}$$

$$CI = (\lambda_{max} - n)/(n - 1) \tag{6}$$

where CR is the random consistency rate of A, CI is the general consistency index, RI is the average random consistency index.

In determining the index weight, to guarantee the objectives and veracity of every weight assignment, this paper refers to consumer survey results, investigation reports of many well-known consulting companies and much counterparts expertise. The paper compares and grades the importance of every two factors in the index hierarchy, then sets a judgement matrix by average importance grades of every index and forms a market competition evaluation hierarchy for the current electric vehicles market.

Results and analysis

In the above analysis based on the vehicle database, EVs in the Chinese market concentrate on mini-cars (A00 class), small cars (A0 class), compact cars (A class) and midsize cars (B class). This paper sorts out vehicle types and contrasts the evaluation indexes of all vehicles in each class, then finds out the position of all evaluation indexes, as Table 3 shows.

Table 3 Indexes features of mini-cars (A00 class), small cars (A0 class), compact cars (A class) and midsize cars (B class)

	A00 class	A0 class	A class	B class
Top speed (km/h)	70–140	120–190	150–180	140–200
Acceleration time (0–100 km/h)	–	10.4–24.8	12–18	8.5–14
Driving range (km)	80–120	100–200	120–250	130–300
Vehicle mass (kg)	1080–1300	1250–1790	1240–1699	1690–1824
Battery capacity (kWh)	10–18.5	16.5–36	18–40	30.4–48
Battery mass (kg)	160–220	167–340	220–395	320–500
Vehicle price (10,000 Yuan)	5–23	9.98–22.8	16.9–26.8	20–36.7
Fuel economy (electricity) (kWh/100 km)	11.6–14	12.1–17.5	11.8–18	15–23
Length (mm)	2695–3600	3708–4445	4502–4670	4560–4861
Width (mm)	1495–1700	1555–1794	1705–2046	1820–1895
Height (mm)	1485–1595	1464–1865	1305–1780	1462–1730
Number of seats	2–4	4	4–5	4–5
Charging time (slow charge) (h)	6–8	7–12	7–12	8–20

Our analysis presents technology level and future development tendency of EV key components, then synthesises the policy goals and the market demand, and finds the regulation of every evaluation index from Table 3. It also forecasts the performance and the cost of mini-cars (A00 class), small cars (A0 class), compact cars (A class) and midsize cars (B class) by electric vehicle dynamic and economic models, and evaluates the market competition of every class in the next 5 years. The results are shown in Figure 7.

Figure 7 Market competitiveness of various EV models

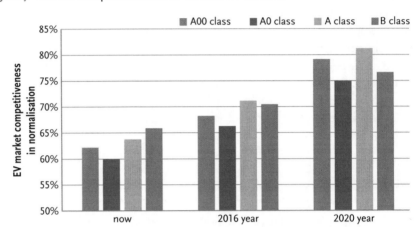

In the present EV market, the competition of B class is stronger. The main reason is that the driving range and dynamic performance of A00 class, A0 class and A class are inadequate. However, the majority of the A00 class holds great superiority in price, and its competitiveness is obvious in a certain market segment. With the development of batteries, motors and other key components of EV technologies, advantages of the B class cars will be gradually weakened in 2016. One important factor is the increasing battery energy density, which extends the EV driving range. Due to the configuring constraints of different class cars, only A class cars catch up with the B class by the improvement of dynamic and comfort performances. In 2020, A class cars keep their comprehensive advantages as the most competitive class, exceeding B class by 5%. Performance deficiencies of A00 class cars are compensated by the increasing technology level. Since the low price has the more obvious advantage, A class cars also catch up with the B class.

Discussion

The characteristics of the Chinese EV market are different from those of the US. The sales of micro-EVs, such as Kandi K10, defined as A00 class EV in this investigation, ranked first by 15,000 in the Chinese market in 2014. This kind of EV is mostly sold by time-sharing lease, which has proved suitable to the Chinese market. This kind of EV only operates in specialist areas, not as a normal EV for ordinary use. Therefore the sales data cannot prove that Aoo class cars are the most competitive. Research on effectiveness of the new business model will be conducted in future. Based on the data for world EV sales, it is obvious that B class cars have advantages due to the additional cost sensitivity. The Nissan Leaf is the most popular EV in the world, of which cumulative sales reached 158,354 by the end of 2014 [19]. The Qichen e30, the Chinese market version of the Nissan Leaf electric car, launched on the Chinese market in November 2014. Most Chinese EV experts regard this car highly and it is forecast to have great potential in the Chinese market. Therefore, our results are in line with the current actual market conditions.

Pure electric vehicles are more difficult to form large-scale markets compared with plug-in electric vehicles due to restrictions in charging infrastructure. Some Chinese mega cities, such as Beijing, place most importance on developing pure electric vehicles because of their zero local emissions in order to solve the problems of smog and haze. More effective policies and continuous technological progress should be made to promote EV penetration. It is recommended that:

► As the Chinese EV market is in the transition phase and consumers are sensitive to price, state subsidy should not be phased out in advance before establishment of the EV mass market for private use.

► For the Chinese government, the construction of charging infrastructure should be accelerated to support EV mass penetration in enough numbers with reasonable distribution; at the same time, the interface and protocol should be unified to maximise utilisation.

► To promote the B class EV, wheelbase could be used as a local subsidy criterion different from that of the state subsidy, which is based on electric range only. In some areas, such as Jiangsu Province, this kind of local subsidy mechanism has been introduced.

► The local and regional protectionist policies need to be effectively discouraged.

► For EV makers, it is important to improve public awareness by commercial promotional activities, such as test drives of EVs and EVs on campus.

► To encourage installation of NCM traction batteries for their high energy density; the mass application will lead to rapid cost decline.

Conclusion

This paper attempts to establish an EV market competitiveness evaluation system on the basis of the new energy vehicles database. The function score method in the elastic search and analytic hierarchy process are used in the evaluation system to obtain the following conclusions:

▶ EVs in the Chinese market are mainly concentrated in mini-cars (Aoo class), small cars (Ao class), compact cars (A class) and midsize cars (B class).

▶ At the current EV technology level, the B Class is the most competitive due to the advantages of dynamic performance. Aoo class cars are also competitive with an obvious price advantage, which is suitable for a subdivided market.

▶ As the EV technology, dynamic and comfort performance of A class cars improve gradually, it is predicted that the market competition of A class will exceed that of B class in 2020 by more than 5%. In addition, performance deficiencies of Aoo class cars are compensated by the price advantage. The market competition of Aoo class is also predicted to exceed the B class.

References

Forman E H, Gass S I. The analytic hierarchy process: an exposition. Operations Research, 2001, 49(4): 469-486.

Hao H, Wang M, Zhou Y, et al. Levelized costs of conventional and battery electric vehicles in China: Beijing experiences. Mitigation and Adaptation Strategies for Global Change, 2014: 1-18.

http://jjs.mof.gov.cn/zhengwuxinxi/tongzhigonggao/201309/t20130916_989833.html

http://www.gov.cn/guowuyuan/2014-07/09/content_2714830.htm

http://www.gov.cn/zhengce/content/2014-07/21/content_8936.htm

http://www.nissan-global.com/EN/NEWS/2015/_STORY/150204-01-e.html?rss

Kammen D M, Arons S M, Lemoine D M, et al. Cost-effectiveness of greenhouse gas emission reductions from plug-in hybrid electric vehicles. Environment, 2002, 7(2): 155-62.

Kuć R, Rogoziński M. Mastering ElasticSearch[M]. Packt Publishing Ltd, 2013.

Lin, Z., et al., User Guide for the ORNL MA3T Model 2012: Oak Ridge National Laboratory.

Minggao Ouyang, Jianqiu Li and Fuyuan Yang, et al. Automotive new powertrain: systems, models and controls. Beijing: Tsinghua University Press, 2008.

Nanaki E A, Koroneos C J. Comparative economic and environmental analysis of conventional, hybrid and electric vehicles—the case study of Greece. Journal of Cleaner Production, 2013, 53: 261-266.

Neubauer J, Brooker A, Wood E. Sensitivity of battery electric vehicle economics to drive patterns, vehicle range, and charge strategies. Journal of Power Sources, 2012, 209: 269-277.

Neubauer J, Wood E. The impact of range anxiety and home, workplace, and public charging infrastructure on simulated battery electric vehicle lifetime utility. Journal of Power Sources, 2014, 257: 12-20.

Ou X, Zhang X, Chang S. Alternative fuel buses currently in use in China: life-cycle fossil energy use, GHG emissions and policy recommendations. Energy Policy, 2010, 38(1): 406-418.

Saaty T L. Decision making with the analytic hierarchy process. International Journal of Services Sciences, 2008, 1(1): 83-98.

Saaty T L. What is the analytic hierarchy process? Springer Berlin Heidelberg, 1988.

Shiau C S N, Samaras C, Hauffe R, et al. Impact of battery weight and charging patterns on the economic and environmental benefits of plug-in hybrid vehicles. Energy Policy, 2009, 37(7): 2653-2663.

Tate E D, Harpster M O, Savagian P J. The electrification of the automobile: from conventional hybrid, to plug-in hybrids, to extended-range electric vehicles. SAE Technical Paper, 2008.

Yu Z, Xia Q. Automobile Theory. China Machine Press, 2009.

DOI: [10.9774/GLEAF.8757.2014.ju.00005]

An Eco-efficiency Assessment Model and System for Automotive Products in China*

Renshu Yin, Yisong Chen, Yanping Yang*,
Linming Xie and Haolan Liao
Hunan University, China

The soaring vehicle population in China has brought more and more pressure on its ecosystem. In order to evaluate the automotive products' eco-efficiency in China quantitatively, the MEP-IA model and Vehicle-IA system were developed. To build up the system, first an MEP-IA (material, energy, pollution–impact assessment) calculation model was designed, by which the automotive products' eco-efficiency could be assessed. Then a database which contained the related Chinese industrial data was established by using the SQL Server. Besides, the background calculation module and multiple user interfaces were designed by using MATLAB and Visual Basic, respectively. Finally, the availability of the system was verified through an empirical study of a power seat as the selected vehicle component, by which its eco-efficiency was calculated and analysed.

● Automotive products

● Eco-efficiency

● MEP-IA model

● Vehicle-IA system

● Power seat

Renshu Yin received his BEng degree in the East China University of Science and Technology in 2006. Currently, he is pursuing his PhD degree at Hunan University. His research interests include life-cycle impact assessment of automotive products, alternative-fuel vehicles and electrical vehicles, and the strategic research of automotive industry in China.

✉ State Key Laboratory of Advanced Design and Manufacturing for Vehicle Body, Hunan University, Changsha 410082, China

🖥 enjoyrenshu@163.com

Yisong Chen received his PhD degree in vehicle engineering from the Hunan University in China in 2014. His research interests include life-cycle assessment of automotive products, system dynamics, liquefied natural gas vehicles, and strategic research into the automotive industry in China.

✉ State Key Laboratory of Advanced Design and Manufacturing for Vehicle Body, Hunan University, Changsha 410082, China

🖥 chenyisong_1988@163.com

Yanping Yang is a professor in the School of Mechanicals & Vehicle Engineering in Hunan University. Her research interests include advanced manufacturing techniques, life-cycle assessment of automotive products, and strategic research into the automotive industry in China.

✉ State Key Laboratory of Advanced Design and Manufacturing for Vehicle Body, Hunan University, Changsha 410082, China

🖥 yyphnu@163.com

* This work was financially supported by the National Nature Science Foundation of China (Grant No: 71173072), the Research Fund for the Doctoral Program of Higher Education of China (Grant No: 20090161110008), the Changsha City Soft Science Research Program (Grant No: K1406040-11) and the Low Carbon Manufacturing of Automotive Products Innovation Team Project of Ningbo (Grant No: 2011B81006).

* Corresponding author.

Linming Xie received his BEng degree at Hunan Normal University in 2013. Currently, he is pursuing his PhD degree at Hunan University. His research interests include life-cycle assessment software developing and greenness ranking for automotive products.

✉ State Key Laboratory of Advanced Design and Manufacturing for Vehicle Body, Hunan University, Changsha 410082, China

🖥 linmingxie11@163.com

Haolan Liao received his MEng degree in engineering mathematics from Ningbo University in 2014. Currently, he is pursuing his PhD degree at Hunan University. His research interests include industry engineering, multi-objective optimization, and uncertainty studies.

✉ State Key Laboratory of Advanced Design and Manufacturing for Vehicle Body, Hunan University, Changsha 410082, China

🖥 liaohaolan@163.com

T HE VEHICLE POPULATION GROWING WITH each passing day has exerted more and more significant impacts on the ecological environment in China. Under the dual pressure of energy and environment, the automotive products which are energy-saving and environment-friendly are becoming competitive in the automobile industry. However, without quantitative life-cycle assessment and reliable results, the government finds it difficult to make related policies, while the auto-makers cannot focus on an adequate technology roadmap; nor can the consumers choose those products that are ecologically friendly. Therefore, it is becoming more and more urgent to develop such a system to evaluate the eco-efficiency of automotive products in China.

There are examples of fully fledged life-cycle assessment software worldwide, such as GaBi, SimaPro, GREET (The Greenhouse Gases, Regulated Emissions, and Energy Use in Transportation), eco-it and so on; but the best part of their data was based on European and US contexts, which was not suitable for Chinese auto-makers and their upstream suppliers. Besides, the software's universal calculation models and relative parameters were not designed specifically for automotive products [1,2]. Therefore, the results and conclusions could hardly guide the automotive products' green design. Meanwhile, the life-cycle assessment's quality and reliability was highly dependent on the data, especially the basic data. Thus, there had been researchers who conducted some explorations and discussions about how to obtain the basic data and how to perform secondary treatment to make the data more precise. For example, Finnveden *et al.* (2009) classified the data into process data and summary data [3]. Dlamini *et al.* (2011) revised the ELCD (European Life-cycle Database) to meet the demands of Australian and Japanese-related empirical studies [4,5]. In China, there were also two widely used databases: CLCD (Chinese Life-cycle Database) of eBalance software from Sichuan University and Sino Center from Beijing University of Technology [6–8]. In this research, the targets and scopes were different, while the methods dealing with basic data statistics were also different, which would result in huge differences in the conclusions even with the same data source.

In this paper, we developed an automotive products eco-efficiency assessment system which can conduct quantitative assessment of automotive products' eco-efficiency for all kinds of automotive products that are made in China. Eco-efficiency includes both ADP (abiotic depletion potential) impact and environmental performances, which converts 'materials-energy' into the unified unit of ADP equivalent for further calculation, and 'environment' into environmental impact equivalent. Based on the previous life-cycle MEP (material-energy-pollution) assessment model developed by the same research team [9,10], we finally established the automotive products eco-efficiency assessment MEP-IA (impact assessment) calculation model. In this model, we only used two equivalents to scale how much the automotive products would impact the environment, for the indicators were simple and thorough, which made the assessment results obvious, concise and easy to promote.

Establishment of the MEP-IA model

The MEP-IA calculation model can calculate the automotive products' ADP equivalent and environmental equivalent in each life-cycle stage respectively, which includes the raw materials producing, components processing and manufacturing, products manufacturing and assembly, running and use of automobile, scrappage and recycling, and the last stage of logistics processes. This calculation model has a strong adaptability which can not only calculate automotive products eco-efficiency in its whole life-cycle but also output the calculation results in one or a few stages; after further improvement, the system can also be applied to other industry products.

ADP calculation model

According to the ISO standards for life-cycle assessment (LCA) [11] and characteristics of automotive products' impact on ADP, the process of ADP is shown as Figure 1.

Figure 1 Process of abiotic depletion potential (ADP) calculation

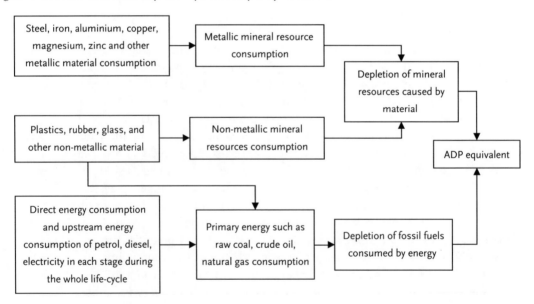

According to the processes of the ADP calculation, the mathematical model of automotive products' ADP equivalent was established.

ADP equivalent factor matrix
First, we built three matrices: MP_1, MP_2 and EP, which were the collections of the ADP coefficients of the metallic materials, the non-metallic mineral resources, and the main kinds of primary energy; where mp_{1ij}, mp_{2ij} and ep_{ij}

represent the ADP coefficient of the ith metallic material, the ith non-metallic mineral resources, and the ith primary energy, respectively.

According to the method proposed by the Leiden University Environmental Science Center (CML), we selected antimony as the reference resource and set its ADP coefficient as the benchmark for the equivalent factor. Thus, we obtained matrix MDP_1 of the metallic materials ADP equivalent factors, matrix MDP_2 of the non-metallic material ADP equivalent factors and matrix EDP of the energy consumption equivalent factors; where mdp_{1ij}, mdp_{2ij} and edp_{ij} are the ADP equivalent factors which were obtained by dividing mp_{1ij}, mp_{2ij} and ep_{ij} by the antimony ADP coefficient.

ADP equivalent calculation

Assuming that k denotes the number of kinds of automotive components; hence metallic materials and non-metallic mineral resources consumption matrices are the $k*n$ order matrix M_B and the $k*n_2$ order matrix M_o, respectively, where element m_{bij} in the matrix means how much the jth metallic material was consumed by the ith component. Then the matrix ADP_1, according to the material consumption, can be expressed as:

$$ADP_1 = M_B \bullet MDP_1 + M_O \bullet MDP_2 \tag{1}$$

Matrix ET, EW, EA, EU, ER and ED denote primary energy consumption in each stage, respectively, from raw materials producing, components processing and manufacturing, products manufacturing and assembly, running and use of automobile, scrap and recycling to the last stage of logistics processes. The dimension of the matrix can be set as order $k*h$ (default value is 'o'); therefore the matrix ADP_2 corresponding to energy consumption could be expressed as:

$$ADP_2 = (ET + EW + EA + EU + ER + ED) \bullet EDP \tag{2}$$

When these two items were added up, the resource depletion equivalent matrix ADP can be obtained as:

$$ADP = ADP_1 + ADP_2 \tag{3}$$

Then the resource depletion equivalent value adp can be calculated by adding all the elements in the matrix up:

$$adp = \sum_{i=1}^{k} (adp_{ij}) \, k \times 1 \tag{4}$$

Environmental impact calculation model

According to the literature [11–14] and specific to the characteristics of automotive products, this paper has selected six types of environmental impact as automotive products environmental impact assessment indices: global warming, acidification, eutrophication, photochemical smog, human health and solid waste. The process is shown in Figure 2.

Figure 2 Process of environmental impact evaluation

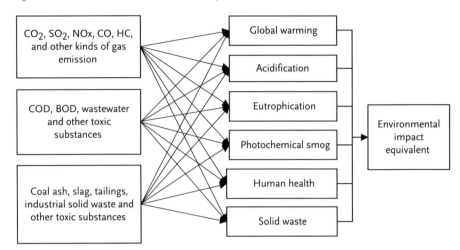

According to the environmental impact processes in Figure 2, we established the calculation model for the automotive products' environmental impact equivalent.

Environmental impact equivalent factor matrices

Taking global warming as an example, we can build the equivalent matrix GWP (global warming potential) which consists of GWP_I and GWP_2. Here gwp_{1ij} stands for the coefficient of environmental impact of global warming caused by the ith gaseous emission, while gwp_{2ij} means the coefficient of environmental impact of global warming caused by the ith toxic and harmful substance. Similarly, we built up the acidification equivalent factor matrix AP, the eutrophication equivalent factor matrix EP, the photochemical smog equivalent factor matrix $POCP$, the body health equivalent factor matrix HTP and the solid waste equivalent factor matrix SW.

Environmental impact equivalent calculation

PT, PW, PA, PU, PR and PD are gaseous emission matrices in each stage, respectively, and their dimension is $k*d$ (default value is '0'). PHT, PHW, PHA, PHU, PHR and PHD are toxic and harmful substance matrices, respectively, their dimension is still $k*e$ (default value is '0'). According to environmental impact equivalent factors we can calculate GW equivalent matrix $IS_{(GWP)}$ as:

$$IS_{(GWP)} = (PT + PW + PA + PU + PR + PD) \bullet GWP_I$$
$$+ (PHT + PHW + PHA + PHU + PHR + PHD) \bullet GWP_2 \qquad (5)$$

In the same way, the six environmental impact equivalent matrices can be constructed. Then the normalisation would be carried out according to their weights. Thus, the automotive products life-cycle environmental impact equivalent matrix AIP can be expressed as follows:

$$AIP = [IS_{(GWP)}, IS_{(AP)}, IS_{(EP)}, IS_{(POCP)}, IS_{(HTP)}, IS_{(SW)}] \bullet (\beta_{ij})_{6\times1} \qquad (6)$$

where $i = 1\text{~}6$ in β_{ij}, respectively, indicates six weight coefficients corresponding to the different types of environmental impact equivalent.

Finally, adding all the elements in matrix AIP together, we get the environmental impact equivalent of automotive products as below:

$$aip = \sum_{i=1}^{k} (aip_{ij}) \, k\times1 \qquad (7)$$

Development of Vehicle-IA system

According to the previously established MEP-IA calculation model, we built up the basic database with SQL Server [15], designed the background calculation engine with MATLAB [16], and then developed diversified interfaces with Visual Basic to achieve the main goal of popularisation [17]. The software system development process of Vehicle-IA is shown in Figure 3.

Figure 3 Software system development process of Vehicle-IA

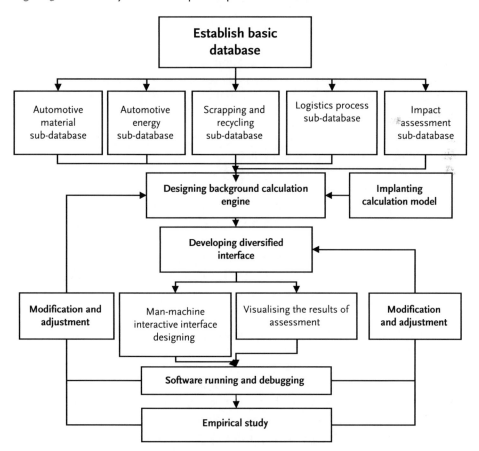

The basic database

Automotive products eco-efficiency assessment depends on a huge amount of basic data and contains much complexity of processes and interactive relationships. Specific to these characteristics, we have applied the correlation model of the SQL Server tool as storage structure; namely, we used a number of two-dimensional tables to store data in which each row is used as a record to describe the message of a certain object and each column as a field to describe the properties of a certain object.

Automotive materials sub-database

All kinds of automotive material in the mining and smelting process will cause energy consumption and pollution emissions, which need to be transformed to ensure the accuracy and practicability of the basic data. Hence, in order to retrieve and call the necessary data in the calculation process efficiently, we have established an automotive materials (such as steel, iron, aluminium and copper) sub-database and once again transformed the data from the Typical Materials and Energy Production Life-cycle Inventory Data from the Beijing University of Technology and the CLCD Database from Sichuan University.

Automotive energy sub-database

There are many types of energy consumption during the automotive life-cycle and the upstream energy production will also bring about energy consumption. Hence, based on the same consideration mentioned before, we have established an automotive energy (such as diesel, gasoline, electricity, natural gas) sub-database and once again transformed the data from the above-mentioned sources.

Scrapping and recycling sub-database

Scrapping and recycling is the most complicated process in the automotive life-cycle, it involves reusing, remanufacturing and recycling (3R); moreover, the means of scrapping and recycling for different components are always different. Therefore, it is becoming more and more important to establish a scrapping and recycling sub-database for the basic data of scrapped vehicle components (such as quantity, weight and recycling property), then this database can be retrieved quickly and all the components can be managed and classified through the 3R method.

Logistics process sub-database

The automotive logistics process mainly includes three categories—components logistics, automobile logistics and reverse logistics—each of which may involve one or more different transport methods such as waterways, roads or railways. In each way it will also bring about energy consumption and emissions. Thus, the sub-database of automotive logistics process was established to collect and manage those energy consumption and emission data for unit mass and unit distance in the three major transportation methods above.

Impact assessment sub-database

Impact assessment is mainly used in environmental and ecological studies, and it is the last step of eco-efficiency assessment. There are many impact assessment approaches, between which the differences are significant. In this study, based on China's actual conditions we have selected the impact factors such as ADP, GWP, POCP and AP in the CML method, which are caused by the major kinds of tailpipe emissions. To establish the impact factor sub-database, those impact factors were collected as basic data and then sorted according to their properties.

The background calculation engine

MATLAB is a software package used in science and engineering calculation. It allows the user to utilise mathematical language to write programmes and provides the interface to the advanced computer languages such as C/C++ and Fortran. It can also realise hybrid programming with Visual Basic by means of ActiveX, matrix library, dynamic-link library, etc. For the automotive products involving a wide range of components, materials, energies and emissions during their whole life-cycle, the calculations in this paper was expressed in the form of matrices and MATLAB was used to design the background calculation engine.

The design of the multiple interfaces is a crucial step in software development, which not only needs to realise the original man-machine interface design but also to visualise the results. In order to facilitate the operation, while taking the auto-maker's requirements into account, we chose Visual Basic as the object-oriented diversified interface development tool; hence, by hybrid programming with Visual Basic, MATLAB and SQL, the system can be operated very easily.

An empirical study

In order to verify and improve the Vehicle-IA model, with assistance from the automotive enterprises, we selected a power seat in production to carry out the empirical study; some data were collected from another study by the same research team [18]. First, we input its inventory such as BOM (bill of materials) table, manufacturing assembly process energy and emission table, usage stage energy consumption table, scrapping and recycling table and logistics table and so on into the system through the interactive interface. Then we called the basic data from SQL and conducted the analytical calculation with the background calculation engine out of the MATLAB work environment. Finally the eco-efficiency assessment results of this power seat were obtained. The power seat's assessing results of ADP equivalent and environmental equivalent calculation were visualised through the diversified interface shown in Figures 4 and 5.

Figure 4 Abiotic depletion potential equivalent calculation results

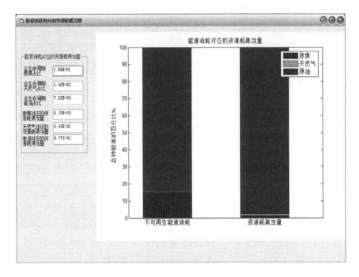

Figure 5 Environmental impact equivalent calculation results

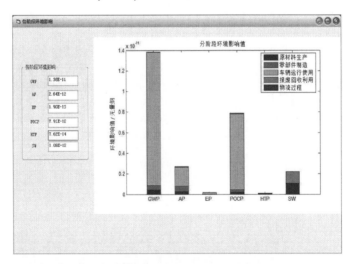

Note: As this software system is developed for Chinese users, its interfaces are mostly in Chinese

Tables 1 and 2 summarise the assessment results of the life-cycle ADP impact and environmental impact.

Table 1 Assessment results of ADP impact for automotive power seats

| Non-renewable resources | Metallic material ADP | | | Non-renewable resource ADP | | |
	AL	Cu	Fe	Raw coal	Natural gas	Crude oil
Consumption quantity (kg)	5.69 E-02	8.25 E-02	6.22	149.86	7.27	850.55
ADP (kg antimony equivalent)	1.44 E-06	2.06 E-04	1.03 E-05	1.21 E-04	7.18 E-05	8.39 E-03
Total (kg antimony equivalent)	2.18 E-04			8.59 E-03		
Total (kg antimony equivalent)	8.81 E-03					

Table 2 Assessment results of environmental impact for automotive power seats (dimensionless)

Phase of life-cycle	Material preparation	Manufacturing phase	Use phase	Scrapping and recycling phase	Logistics process	Total
GWP	4.5131 E-13	4.2397 E-13	1.2897 E-11	3.0897 E-14	3.5058 E-15	1.3807 E-11
AP	2.8137 E-13	5.1072 E-13	1.9126 E-12	−6.3136 E-14	2.6425 E-15	2.6442 E-12
EP	1.283 E-14	2.1849 E-14	1.6353 E-13	−3.8501 E-15	1.4419 E-16	1.9454 E-13
POCP	2.0188 E-13	2.4429 E-13	7.3809 E-12	8.8167 E-14	1.4255 E-15	7.9166 E-12
HTP	1.5913 E-14	8.6542 E-15	5.8311 E-14	−6.7166 E-015	5.6509 E-17	7.6219 E-14
SW	2.1429 E-12	2.3777 E-14	4.3621 E-14	−1.1289 E-12	7.6512 E-17	1.0814 E-12
Total	2.5715 E-11					

According to Tables 1 and 2, we can find the results discussed below.

The consumption of non-renewable resources for current power seats is far greater than the consumption of renewable energy. Among the non-renewable resources, the consumption of raw coal and crude oil is much higher than that of natural gas, which is determined by the current energy consumption structure of China. In the future, we should generalise the use of cleaner energies such as natural gas and gradually make use of wind energy, hydropower and other renewable energy sources. The mass of copper (Cu) only accounts for 1.30%

of total metallic material consumption, but its ADP accounts for 94.6% of the total. The addition of motors to motor vehicle seats leads to a significant increase of the ADP. Thus, we suggest substituting a metal with lower ADP for copper (Cu) in power seat motors.

The environmental impact equivalent in the use phase is far greater than the other phases. Meanwhile, GWP is the largest of the six environmental impacts. In the future, improving vehicle technology to reduce CO_2 is the most important way to cut down the environmental impact equivalent in the whole life-cycle. The equivalent in the scrapping and recycling phases is negative, thus scrapping and recycling is the most important way to reduce environmental impacts in the full life-cycle of power seats. With continuous improvements in recycling and green design technologies, if we can remanufacture and reuse the power seats and make full use of recycled energy from burning non-metallic materials, there will be great potential for reducing the total environmental impact index of power seats.

Conclusion and discussion

In this paper, with multidisciplinary knowledge from automotive engineering, environmental science and computer science, among others, we established the MEP-IA model and developed the Vehicle-IA system, which is an eco-efficiency assessment methodology more suitable for China's actual situation. In the future, the study could be improved in the following directions.

▶ During system development, some data interfaces had been reserved which can access the basic database, background calculation engine and the multiple-user interface. Hence, after analysing the empirical application and according to the different problems encountered in the actual operation process, the system could be optimised in many ways such as database upgrading and extending, optimisation of calculation efficiency and communicating and intelligent and diverse graphical output. The system can not only be used for automotive enterprises to make greener products but also provide some references to automotive energy saving and emission reduction for those standard-makers.

▶ The effects of the automotive components on the ecological environment involve many dynamic factors. Thus, the evaluation only from a static point of view will be inevitably relatively isolated and one-sided, thus resulting in a significant reduction of the reference value. However, most current studies still remain in the static phase, with a lack of dynamic simulation and analysis. Therefore, the systems theory approach is required to provide a multi-perspective and all-around dynamic assessment for the eco-efficiency of the automotive components regarding the differences in the natural resources, the industrial structures and the economic development levels for various times and various regions. Then, the ecological impact caused by a variety of techniques can be forewarned, and scientific references can be provided for the path selection of the enterprise technique upgrade and the decision-making of government.

References

SimaPro: World's Leading LCA Software. http://www.pre-sustainability.com/simapro

Product Sustainability Software: GaBiSoftware. http://www.gabi-software.com/international/index/

Finnveden G, Hauschild M Z, Ekvall T, et al. Recent developments in Life-cycle Assessment. Journal of Environment Management, 2009, 91: 1-21

Puri P, Compston P, Pantano V. Life-cycle assessment of Australian automotive door skins. The International Journal of Life-cycle Assessment, 2009, 14: 420-428

Dlamini N G, Fujimura K, Yamasue E, et al. The environmental LCA of steel vs HDPE car fuel tanks with varied pollution control. The International Journal of Life-cycle Assessment, 2011, 16: 410-419

Liu Xialu, Wang Hongtao, Chen Jian, 2010. Method and basic model for development of Chinese reference life-cycle database. Journal of Environmental Science, 30(10), 2136-2144

Huang Na, Wang Hongtao, Fan Ci, et al., 2012. LCA data quality assessment and control based on uncertainty and sensitivity analysis. Journal of Environmental Science, 32(6), 1529-1536.

Wang H T, Hou P, et al., 2011 A Novel Weighting Method in LCIA and its Application in Chinese Policy Context. Matthias Finkbeiner. In Towards Life-cycle Sustainability Management (Berlin: Springer), 65-72.

Tu Xiaoyue, Yang Yanping, Xu Jianquan, et al., 2013. Evaluation of difference between LNG and diesel heavy-duty commercial vehicle's life-cycle environmental emission. China Mechanical Engineering, 24(11), 1525-1530.

Tu Xiaoyue, Xu Jianquan, Chen Yisong, et al., 2013. An evaluation of difference between the LNG and diesel commercial vehicle's life-cycle energy consumption. China Mechanical Engineering, 24(23), 3211-3215

Guinée, J.B. et al. Handbook on life-cycle assessment. Operational guide to the ISO standards. I: LCA in perspective. IIa: Guide. IIb: Operational annex. III: Scientific background. Kluwer Academic Publishers, Dordrecht, 2002

Gu Lijing. Studies on the Environmental Impact of the Building Industry in China based on the Life-cycle Assessment. Beijing: Tsinghua University, 2009

Yang Qianmiao. Quantificational Life-cycle Assessment of Environmental Impact of Construction Productions. Tianjin: Tianjin University, 2009

Liu Zheng. Research on environmental consciousness design and evaluation method of electromechanical products. Hangzhou: Zhejiang University, 2013

Zhang Limin. Research center. SQL Server Examples of database development. Beijing: Machinery Industry Press, 2005.

Kong Xian, Xu Liumei. MATLAB7.0 Basic Tutorial. Beijing: Tsinghua University Press, 2005

Zhang Xianku. VB practical programming techniques from basic to development. Dalian: Dalian University of Technology Press, 1997.

Yisong Chen, Yanping Yang, Xiang Li, Haibo Dong & Ruibin Bai. Life-cycle resource consumption of automotive power seats, International Journal of Environmental Studies, (2014) 71:4, 449-462

DOI: [10.9774/GLEAF.8757.2014.ju.00006]

Community-Based Mobility Services as Part of a Sustainable Transport System for Suburban China

The Example of Shared Shuttles (*banche*) in Shanghai*

Ting Sun and Jean-François Doulet

Paris School of Urban Planning (University of Paris East)/Lab'Urba, France

- Suburbanisation
- Urban transport
- Community-based mobility services
- Shared shuttles (*banche*)
- Shanghai

Our research aims at identifying collective forms of transportation that could support sustainable mobility in Chinese cities. Taking the case of Shanghai, we focus on the analysis of shared shuttles (*banche*, in Chinese): shuttle bus services that are being operated locally by private entities, such as owners' committees, companies or hypermarkets. Based on interviews with users, operators and officials, we analyse how those community-based services succeed in addressing mobility needs in suburban areas. We think that integrating them into a comprehensive urban transport strategy could be beneficial to the efficiency of the overall urban mobility system. We make propositions to improve the performance of those shared shuttles.

Ting Sun is a PhD Candidate at the Paris School of Urban Planning (University of Paris East)/Lab'Urba, France. Her thesis examined the development and evolution of informal transport in Chinese cities.

✉ Cité Descartes - bâtiment Bienvenüe - plot A,14-20, bld Newton, Champs sur Marne, 77454 Marne la Vallée cedex 2
Paris Institute of Urban Planning (University of Paris East)/Lab'Urba, France

🖥 sunny168816@gmail.com

Jean-François Doulet, PhD, is an associate professor at the Paris School of Urban Planning (University of Paris East)/Lab'Urba, France. He has been researching urban mobility issues in China for more than 20 years. Jean-Francois is the co-director of the Sino-French Centre for Urban, Regional and Planning Studies (created in partnership with Nanjing University). He was previously the head of the China Programme for the Institut pour la ville en mouvement/PSA Peugeot-Citroën (www.city-on-the-move.com).

✉ Cité Descartes - bâtiment Bienvenüe - plot A,14-20, bld Newton, Champs sur Marne, 77454 Marne la Vallée cedex 2
Paris Institute of Urban Planning (University of Paris East)/Lab'Urba, France

🖥 jean-francois.doulet@u-pec.fr

* This research has benefited from financial support from the China Scholarship Council.

Researching community-based mobility services in China

Shuttle buses, paratransit and the notion of community-based mobility services: an international perspective

THE INTERNATIONAL SCIENTIFIC LITERATURE GIVES us some hints to define mobility solutions that are located in a 'grey zone' between personal car and public transport. In the early 1970s, the term paratransit was coined to define collective transportation solutions that are mainly based on shuttle buses to address local and specific mobility needs in contexts where public transportation is absent or not relevant; such a notion paved the way for investigation into non-conventional types of transportation offer in cities (Kirby et al., 1974). As a general term, paratransit can have several dimensions; one of the most important is its decentralised mode of operation: shuttle buses operated in paratransit are mostly community-based mobility services as they are operated by local players—most of the time not institutional—and they address the needs of a community—most of the time a residential area. In several Western countries, paratransit has been supported by public policies. From the late 1980s, in the USA, special neighbourhood mobility programmes have been organised by non-profit organisations or initiated through government assistance to improve the accessibility of inner-city residents to suburban job opportunities (Cervero, 1997). In England, community transport has been defined as: 'Local passenger transport provision which is not provided through scheduled bus or rail services, which is organised on a non-profit basis by voluntary organisations, community transport groups, and other non-statutory bodies' (Department for Transport, 2005). In French-speaking European countries, such mobility services are called *Transports semi-collectifs* (semi-collective transports) or *Transport à la demande* (transport on demand) and are mostly operated in suburban areas where the cost of operating public buses is too high because of low demographic density (Rathery, 1979). In the literature, paratransit solutions are identified as efficient transportation solutions as they can support a collective form of mobility that could become a genuine alternative to private cars. Recent studies have analysed the positive impacts of shared vehicles through car sharing schemes: shared vehicles are more resource efficient and less space consuming than private cars (Firnkorn and Müller, 2012). Besides, people enrolled in car sharing programmes are more likely to use cars less intensively than private car owners (Sioui et al., 2010).

Studying community-based services in China and the key role played by shuttle buses

In China, community-based services also have a rather long history. During the Maoist Era—1950s, 1960s and 1970s—big employers (or work units)[1] were

---

1 *Danwei*, in Chinese

systematically delivering transportation services for their employees as these organisations were managed as paternalistic entities. Shuttles buses (*banche*) started to transport people from home to their workplace and back. Despite the economic and social transformation started in the 1980s, those transportation services have not disappeared (Doulet J.-F., 2005). Chinese cities, especially big cities such as Beijing, Shanghai, and Guangzhou, have experienced rapid growth, resulting in urban expansion and a large increase in population. The development of huge areas of residential settlements in the fringes of cities[2] provides great pressure on urban public transport, especially in suburban areas (Hua and Xu, 2002). The gap between limited public transport offers and increasing demands for mobility is calling for flexible and efficient mobility solutions, especially in suburban areas (Pan H. and Doulet J.-F., 2010). To solve the problem of daily travel from these suburban neighbourhoods to other parts of the city, local players tend to spontaneously organise their own shuttles to meet daily travel. Today, shuttle buses are still operated by companies but also by hypermarkets and owners' committees.[3] A hypermarket shuttle, as another form of shared shuttle, is an important element to attract customers. A hyper-market serves residents within a radius of 3–4 km, if shuttle transport lines are operated, it will attract more people within a radius of 10 km maximum. Each shuttle line reaches one or several neighbourhoods. Neighbourhood shuttles are operating as a bus-sharing mode as they are open to anyone; they are organ-ised by a car leasing company in relation with owners' committees to determine the schedules and routes (Tang and Liu, 2010). Shuttle bus services in China as community-based services can be questioned in many ways: what does their decentralised mode of operation tell us about bottom-up mechanisms in the making of daily services in Chinese cities? How sustainable are those mobil-ity services? How efficient are they in answering unmet mobility needs? What would be the opportunities for public transport policies to integrate them in an overall city strategy? In a context of growing motorisation, it is legitimate to ask if those mobility services could become a genuine alternative and element of a sustainable urban transport system in the future.

Research methodology

As shuttle bus services still remain largely unexplored in academic research, we had to develop an original methodology. We decided to conduct field research, taking Shanghai as a case study; in this city, community-based transport has developed significantly since the late 1990s. To deepen our analysis, we chose to study an area in Shanghai's southwest suburbs where, in comparison to other parts of the city, community-based transport seems to be more developed. This area is characterised by commercial buildings and high-density residential

---

2 Normally, these huge residential areas include several relatively small residential quarters; each one of them has around 10,000 to 40,000 residents.

3 Owners' committees are associations of residents in charge of managing residential quarters.

quarters developed around a metro station (line 1). Our on-site methodology is based on in-depth interviews with users of community-based transport, with residents working for owners' committees, with members of residents' committees who participate in the organisation of the service, with professionals in car leasing companies who operate community-based transport and with officials from the Shanghai municipal transportation commission. Face-to-face interviews were conducted in August 2013 and in January 2014. In August, five small group (three people) interviews were conducted with two owners' committees, two residents' committees and one car leasing company. Thirty-five users in residential quarters agreed to answer our detailed questions about community-based transport. To get strategic insights into the current and future status of community-based transport, we conducted interviews with officials of the Shanghai municipality who introduced the current situation and expressed government opinions. In January, another five interviews with small groups of three people were conducted with two owners' committees, two residents' committees and one car leasing company; twenty-six users around the metro station were surveyed; ten officials agreed to be interviewed. This research aims at proposing an analysis of ongoing changes in urban mobility practices, by exploring the role of community-based transport in the public transport system and by understanding community, organisational and regulatory environments in which community-based transport takes place as a bottom-up solution.

Descriptive analysis of shuttle bus services in Shanghai

Mapping operators of community-based shuttle services

There are no official documents or publications for community-based services, due to the fact that they are partly informal. Two steps were composed for collecting basic data. First of all, all information about community based transport were collected from social websites (such as http://www.fang.com) which are used by local residents to communicate with each other and by owners' committees to publish their official documents. This resulted in identifying neighbourhoods where community-based services were operated. We concluded that, at the end of 2010, more than 50 residential quarters in Shanghai organised their shuttle services. As a confirmation check, we visited those areas to validate the existence of a community-based transport operation; their spatial distribution is shown on Figure 1.

Figure 1 Location of neighbourhoods operating community shuttles in Shanghai (metro lines in red)

According to information from supermarkets and hypermarkets' official websites, at the end of 2006, Shanghai had 112 supermarkets or hypermarkets belonging to 15 different brands, 98 hypermarkets with over 840 shuttle lines and more than 1,000 vehicles. Until 2013, Shanghai had around 900 lines of hypermarkets shuttles compared to 1,120 regular bus lines. The travel distance of each line ranges from 2 km to 38 km. Each shuttle was supporting around 500 trips per day. Figure 2 shows the location of a selection of those supermarkets and hypermarkets.

Figure 2 Location of hypermarkets belonging to three different brands (Carrefour, Locus and Tesco) and their service area in Shanghai

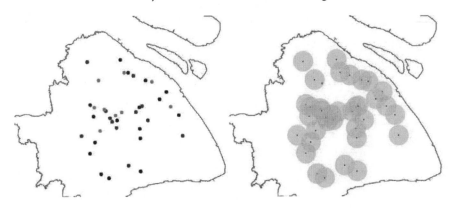

General characteristics of shuttle bus services in Shanghai

Shuttle services have three main functions:

▶ **Specific destination.** This service is always produced for a specific purpose: for example, in the direction of a hypermarket, employment centres such as an industrial park, a company, or a location in the centre of the city. Normally, the journey is 40 minutes long to arrive at an employment centre or a city centre, but less than 20 minutes to the hypermarket

▶ **Feeder service or exchange.** This service provides links to public transport. In most cases, a bus or minibus provides an interchange service at the subway station

▶ **Network service and several organisers.** If an area is served by two or three operators, it is possible to change from a bus line of one operator to a bus line of another. This can create a network of paratransit services. This network service was not designed intentionally, but it exists and is well used by residents when several services are running simultaneously in an area

Figure 3 shows the main types and characteristics of community-based shuttle services in Shanghai: a) several shuttles in the different residential quarters for one metro station, or several shuttles for one hypermarket; b) service between residential quarter and employment centre; and c) network service and more than two organisers.

Figure 3 The three main types of shuttle bus services in Shanghai

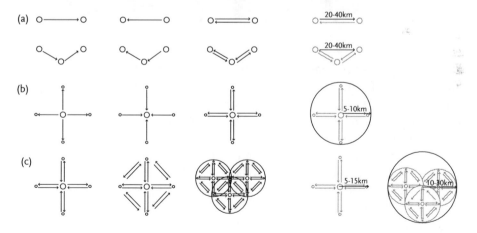

A case study in the southwest suburbs of Shanghai

To understand the operation and performance of shared shuttles, we chose an example in the town of Xinqiao, Songjiang district, located in the southwest of Shanghai's suburbs (see Fig. 4 for location). In 1997, metro line 1 of Shanghai opened its last station in the town of Xinzhuang, next to the town of Xinqiao.

Between 1997 and 2013, around 40 new residential quarters were built in those two towns, attracting about 300,000 new residents. The problems faced by the inhabitants in their daily mobility appeared gradually due to lack of convenient public transport. A low frequency and a short operation time motivated the spontaneous operation of shared shuttles that can quickly meet the demand of people. The owners' committee established with the support of the residents' committee[4] organised shared shuttles to facilitate the daily travel of their residents. We will give details about these two committees and their organisations.

Figure 4 Location of our study area around Xinzhuang metro station

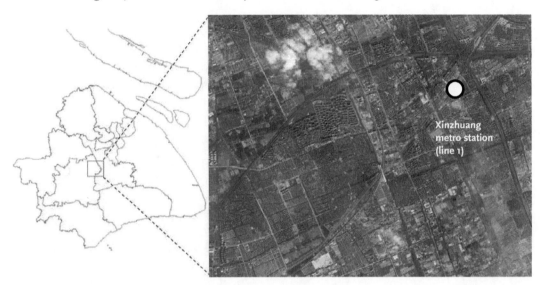

Figure 5 shows that many shared shuttles are operated between Xinzhuang station on metro line 1 and several neighbourhoods. In total, 20 residential quarters are served by these shared shuttle services to facilitate residents' travel to the metro station. Normally, shuttles operate between 6:30 a.m. and 10:00 p.m. Frequency of service is high in the morning between 7:00 and 8:00, and in the evening between 5:30 and 7:00: around 10–15 minutes between buses. In the other parts of the day, some neighbourhoods do not provide services because there are few users. Others extend the time to 15–60 minutes between buses, this way offering a continuous service. Neighbourhood shuttles can carry around 3,600 trips during the morning and the evening every day; for the other parts of the day, about 1,700 trips are carried out by shared shuttles.

---

4 Residents' committees are local administrative bodies in charge of managing daily issues.

Figure 5 Public bus line (left) and neighbourhood shared shuttles (right)

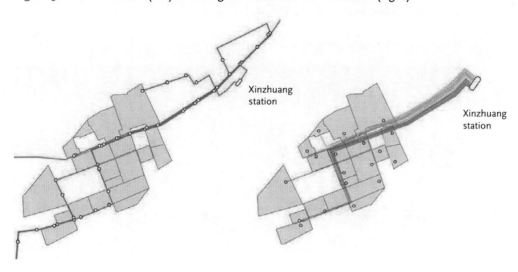

In the same area, a hypermarket tries to attract these residents with the organisation of their own shuttle service (see Figure 6). According to the hypermarket managers we interviewed, the shuttle service is not only a tool to transport people. It is also supposed to influence residents' daily life and change their shopping habits. In the same area, four hypermarkets hold 32 shuttle lines and serve directly more than 80 neighbourhoods with about 0.4–0.5 million residents. Around 18,000–21,000 trips are carried out every day by shared shuttles totally free of charge.

Figure 6 Hypermarket shuttle service network

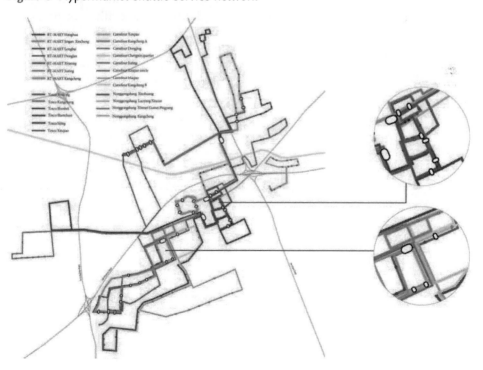

According to our observations on site, the types of vehicles used as shuttles are quite varied: minibus, microbus, bus, etc. (see Fig. 7).

Figure 7 Examples of vehicles used as shared shuttles

Analytical analysis of shuttle bus services in Shanghai

Comparative advantages

Community-based shuttle services have been developed for the last 15 years. The shuttle operation matures progressively along with communication between the residents, the owners' committee, and the management company. Its service is so practical and cannot be replaced directly by regular bus operation because it is based on flexibility and negotiation. The advantages of community-based transport can be summarised as follows (see Table 1):

▶ The schedule and route can be modified through an agreement between residents and operators

▶ Shuttles are operated as 'private buses': their routes link key places useful for local residents. Types and sizes of vehicles depend on needs

▶ Location of bus stops are discussed and decided beforehand and their number is usually less than for a regular bus service

▶ The price of a shuttle ride may be lower than the usual bus for the same distance

▶ Most of the customers live in the same neighbourhoods so they know each other well

Table 1 Shared shuttles compared with other modes of transport

	Speed (km/h)	Number of seats	Advantages	Disadvantages
Bus	16–25	20–50	Large capacity, low cost, low energy consumption per inhabitant, less polluting	Fixed timetable, less comfortable
Shared shuttles	16–25	20–50	Large capacity, low cost, low energy consumption per inhabitant more flexible, more comfortable, more accessible, less polluting	More time for organisation, reservation made in advance, less security, less safety
Taxi	30–40	1–4	Faster, more flexible, more comfortable, more accessible	Low capacity, high costs, more polluting, large ground for operation and parking
Private car	30–40	1–5	More flexible, more comfortable, more accessible	Low capacity, high cost, more polluting, large ground for operation and parking

Local organisation and modes of operation

Neighbourhood shuttles as a mode of spontaneous transport are organised by the cooperation of the owners' committee, the committee of residents, facilities management and car leasing companies. Each participant plays a different role in the process. The residents' committee as the smallest government administrative organisation manages all affairs of the community. The owners' committee is established with the support of the residents' committee. It is an autonomous organisation of the inhabitants to encourage community participation (Fei, 2001). These two organisations are essential for organising and managing neighbourhood shuttles. Although hypermarket shuttles are organised by hypermarkets and car leasing companies, if they expect to travel inside a neighbourhood or make stops inside or close to the door of the residential quarters, they have to arrange it with a residents' committee and owners' committee. These two types of shuttle services serve the residential quarters directly, and their operation is influenced by community participation.

Figure 8 shows the strategic role played by the residents' committee: on the one hand, it is a representative of the city government in the community, giving support to programmes launched by the government; on the other hand, it develops locally several activities and programmes for the residents of the community in a participation process. The emergence and development of the owners' committees are not only changing the structure of the original community governance, but also increasing the complexity of relations within a community, supporting the reform of community governance. Each community has a communication platform on the Internet, so that many residents can communicate simultaneously and everyone can express their opinions quickly. Residents' committees and owners' committees can also publish their official information.

Figure 8 Organisational structure of a residents' committee in Shanghai

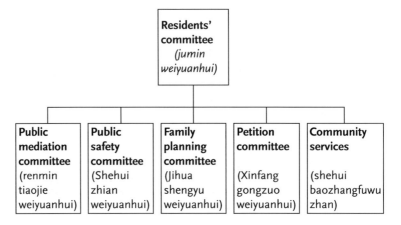

Figure 9 shows the process of the organisation of neighbourhood shuttles. The owners' committee may initiate calls for tenders to choose a facility management company that will manage all matters related to the shuttle service. The owners' committee shall report the result of the organisation to the residents' committee and the local transportation office. The residents' committee supervises the operation of the shuttle by their public mediation committee. If there are accidents or conflicts related to the shuttle bus service, the residents' committee and the owners' committee must reconcile the contradictory needs and expectations. Figure 10 shows that, for hypermarket shuttles, operators have to negotiate with the owners' committee and residents' committee to let them operate in the neighbourhood and discuss the timetable and routes.

Figure 9 Bottom-up organisation of a neighbourhood shuttle service

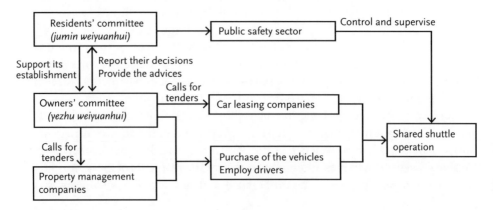

Figure 10 Bottom-up organisation of a hypermarket shuttle bus service

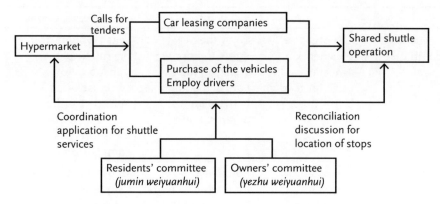

Potential for improvement

Community-based services appear to be a mobility solution particularly well-adapted to the changing needs of the people in the suburbs of Shanghai. However, it is not an independent element out of the entire public transport system. Indeed, it must be encompassed as a complementary element of traditional public transport. The main challenge faced by shared shuttles in the city of Shanghai is the role that they could play in the overall transportation system. Table 2 shows the perceptions and opinions of different participants on community-based transport, according to interviews that we conducted. It appears that there is no clear legislative and regulatory framework dealing with community-based transport. Community-based transport is never taken into account in the public transport system. Regular transport system and shared shuttles are run in parallel without any thought about limiting overlaps. As shuttle services are not regulated by the government, their mode of operation can be questionable. To reduce operating costs, shuttles use the old bus company vehicles. Most of the drivers of shuttles are not officially trained by the transport office. Many shuttles do not have a passenger transport licence. All these elements support the need to establish a regulatory framework to improve the quality and efficiency of community-based transport services.

Table 2 Perceptions and opinions of different players involved in shuttle bus services

Sector		Current role	Key points	Future expectations
Transport organisers and providers	Owners committee	To organise residents' meeting Call for tenders	Enjoy their civil rights to improve quality of life Lots of institutional barriers for organisation	Legal support from the municipal transportation commission Subsidies or funds from the municipal transportation commission
	Community transport operator Car leasing company	To establish contract with owners' committee To operate community transport service for the general public or specific groups	Potential market for long-term rental Worry about the semi-legal operation Cooperation with owners' committee that is growing	To open market for long-term rental services for community-based transport Privatisation of public transport Technology (software for smartphones or information platforms)
Users	General public Special users	To meet the market niche demand Take larger market demand	To enjoy the advantages of community transport To not worry about safety, security and insurance problems because of a semi-illegal operation	A more intelligent and flexible transport service A transport service connected to telephone or internet
Governmental and institutional organisations	Municipal transportation commission Transport planning department Transport regulatory department	No role (there is no planning for community-based transport) Imperfect permit and licence system	To understand and try to accept alternative transport concept Lack of a whole consideration between community transport and public transport Lack of a whole institutional and regulatory framework for community-based transport	Integration with the public transport system Transformation to sustainable and flexible transport There will be a chance to open a part of the market to public transport operation

Continued

Sector		Current role	Key points	Future expectations
	Residents' committee Public service sector Public safety sector	To make decision with owners' committee To report to transport department	To encourage public participation for residential quarter autonomy Need legal support from city level	Legal support from municipal transportation commission Reinforce their responsibility in process of transport organisation and operation

Key challenges for the future of shared shuttles in China

Although shared shuttle services rapidly meet residents' needs for transportation and complement the regular bus system, complex problems are still occurring mainly because they are informal. The current regulatory system for transport obviously cannot adapt the development of the informal bus sector. Until now, community-based transport still has not found a suitable place within the transport legal framework and within a regulatory framework, even though its influence in the overall urban transport system is growing. We can identify three main challenges for community-based transport as a bottom-up solution in the future.

A lack of integration into urban transport systems

Between the 1990s and the beginning of the 2000s, because of the rapid expansion of cities and the development of the automobile industry coupled with massive investments in urban road infrastructures, residents of suburban China were mainly dependent on private cars or regular public transport in their daily life (Goethals, 2011). However, public transport was not always efficient, and ownership of private cars was still limited to relatively affluent people. Today, shuttle buses, carpooling schemes and public bicycle services are forming a new category of mobility services (Pan and Author, 2010). However, more modes of transport does not mean a more efficient transport system. Coordination between different means of transport is one of the key points of development of sustainable transport (Certu, 2009). For community-based transport, there will be the question of integration and intermodality with regular public transport.

An informal solution in search of a more formal future

Due to the fragmented nature of the informal transport sector (Cervero and Golub, 2007), many private operators make it difficult to come out with a unique regulatory framework (Schalekamp and Behrens, 2010). None of the informal operators has responsibility for ensuring the effective function of global road transport. Fiercer competition is being generated if regular bus transport operates the same routes as community-based transport. A large number of informal transport operations will also lead to a higher level of congestion during peak hours. In the current situation, there is also no coordination between conventional bus transport service and informal transport service. Therefore, there is a need to think about the evolution and future direction of community-based transport: will it be formalised by government authority that holds a monopoly for formal bus operation? The main advantage of this public monopoly is that it allows the government to exercise strict control over public services, and easily integrate fares and cooperation between the buses and other modes of transport, especially the metro. However, as the bus service is a non-profitable sector, the government should be responsible for balancing between large subsidies and cost recovery. Will community-based transport as a bottom-up solution with residents' comprehensive opinions be neglected due to the prohibition and strict control of private operation under this situation or will there be an open market for delegation of personal transport for the future? Private operators could find their niche market to complete the formal bus service and meet individual demand for transportation that will not be satisfied by government authority.

A need for a better adapted institutional framework

If community-based transport needs to have a suitable place in the public transport system, the first important thing is to transform the institutional framework that leads to effective transportation management. Several transport authorities are related to informal transport, but none of them as a major authority makes relevant laws and provides effective regulation. These administrations have to tolerate the operation of informal transport to integrate them into the public transport system as a new bottom-up solution. However, unclear attitudes from local government lead to an indistinct institutional framework for community-based transport. For the city of Shanghai, market entry for the car leasing sector is controlled at the same time by the transportation commission and the industrial and commercial administration because of opening the market and re-controlling the market during the 1990s to 2000s. Either of the two permissions of these two government administrations is valid legally. However, to obtain a permit from the transportation commission is much more difficult: this created unfair business competition. Meanwhile, other companies registered by the industrial and commercial administration are not constrained by the conditions given by the transportation commission. In the end, the cost to enter the market is relatively lower than that of companies registered by the transportation commission.

Propositions for planners and policy-makers

Making shared shuttles an element of an intermodal transport strategy

Intermodality means combining several means of transport for the same journey and offering a door-to-door service. As a keystone for sustainable mobility, intermodality is already used for long trips at a metropolitan scale: for example, Hongqiao multimodal exchange hub in Shanghai includes an airport. At a local scale or at a community scale in suburban areas and in towns in suburban Shanghai, intermodal trips have been organised by residents themselves through combining community-based transport and metro services, but these practices of intermodality still have their limits. Public authorities could play a key role in the process of connecting and coordinating different modes of transport in the future. They will need to plan an overall development strategy for integrating different modes of transport and necessary equipment. They will also need to establish a platform with local transport data for large and small transport operators, organisations and travellers. Intermodal pricing or inter-operator ticketing systems will be another essential element to achieve the coordination of transport (Auer, 2012). With one single ticket, travellers will freely take several means of transport. For the future, real-time information about travel time, waiting time, time to go from one transportation mode to another, precise price for each part of the journey will ease intermodal mobility.

To make those measures efficient, there is work to be done on combining the local scale and the metropolitan scale. Since each type of shuttle runs in a different part of the overall public transportation system, the methods for transport integration are different. Figure 11 shows that one possibility is to share the corridors with public transport. Buses and shuttles are operated in the same way by separating traffic space. Another option is to preserve their own corridor, then buses and shuttles will run in parallel. This mode can be used to operate shuttles with large capacities and long distances. Another possibility is to define the operating shuttle area and separate the functions of buses and shuttles. In this mode, the shuttle provides feeder services to the metro station or other public transport spot. As most of the shared shuttles are operated in residential areas close to metro stations, this mode can reduce congestion in major roads. Moreover, to improve the overall transportation system and to reduce congestion, an important approach could be to separate the operation time. During peak hours, shuttle buses may be operated as formal buses to limit their flexibility and strengthen their frequencies, especially for those that work as feeders to main transportation hubs.

Figure 11 Two possible modes of integration: 'operating shuttle area' (left) and 'shuttle corridor' (right)

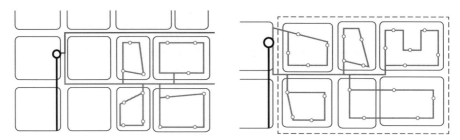

Transforming the institutional framework

Public participation and transportation policy-making could be viewed as a process of interaction. Each of their aspects will help sustainable transportation efforts in the future (Schiller *et al.*, 2010). In many Western countries, community-based transport as a bottom-up solution has involved a public participation process since the late 1990s. However, this bottom-up solution will need to be recognised by policy-makers who should provide a good environment for better development. Besides, the process of implementing intermodality also depends mainly on political will (European Commission, 2004).

Although residents' committees have been involved in the management of community-based transport in China, their function is still limited to providing advice and mediating residents' conflicts. Thus, we could consider that a top-down control and management framework from both the transportation and urban planning municipal commissions could help integrate the entire informal transport sector in a city (Tang and Liu, 2010). Figure 12 shows that the municipal transportation commission, as a major regulatory administration, should establish a registration and permit system to control and conduct the development of community-based transport. Several steps could be proposed through legal and regulatory mechanisms to transform the informal transport system under the context of future Chinese transport regulation:

- ▶ Legalisation of community-based transport service. Shared shuttle service of community-based transport has to be accepted as a legal public transport by the road transportation act in the future

- ▶ The establishment of a dedicated system for registrations, permits and licences. A department of municipal transportation commission could be responsible for the registration of shared shuttles or minibus-taxi associations, their operators and vehicles. Route-based permits or radius-based permits system could be introduced to identify the areas or the routes in which they are allowed to operate

- ▶ Training programmes for advanced driving techniques, minibus management, and customer care could be carried out to enhance standards of operation

► A shuttle service fund composed of the government allowance or a share of the earnings of operators will contribute to the improvement of operation techniques and the quality of vehicles

► Transport policy that encourages the integration of community-based transport systems within the public transport systems

Figure 12 Bottom-up organisation of neighbourhood shuttles

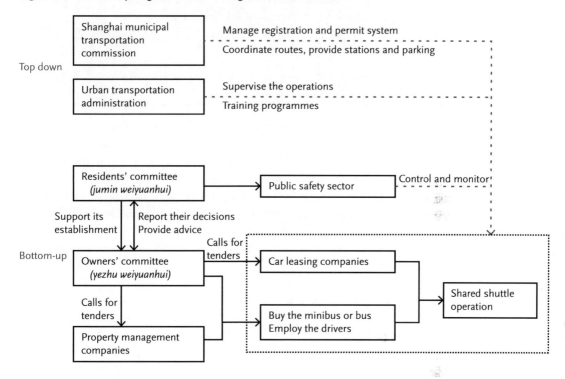

Creating a specific market for community-based transport

Currently, the majority of community-based transport services are operated by car leasing companies through tenders organised by owners' committees. Currently, a reform is pushing towards the opening of the public transport sector to private operators. After several reforms, from nationalisation to privatisation in the 1990s and finally renationalisation in 2000, the Chinese formal bus sector is still dominated by monopolies: contracts are awarded to local public companies without tenders (Ken, 2007). More reforms of the public transport sector may happen in the future. However, the situation of monopoly has its inherent problems. Due to the lack of competition, employees of the public transport sector always have little incentive to increase productivity and to improve service quality. Public enterprises have limited capacity to satisfy every customer since they have to consider the question of public equality and development strategy at the city level. This context offers an opportunity for private operators: they could target real local demand at the community level. Therefore, we propose the creation of a separated market for community-based transport, i.e. different approaches for different markets. In such a context, community-based transport could be always provided by private operators and monitored by the municipal transport commission, residents' committee and owners' committee in the future; it will then be operated in a different market than the regular bus sector that is operated by public enterprises. Car leasing companies could still act as the main suppliers. The municipal transport commission could provide the permit regulation for leasing companies and the licence system for vehicles and drivers to support their operations in a legalised framework.

Concluding remarks

Shared shuttles appear to be a central element of daily mobility in China. In the city of Shanghai, they support a better connectivity of the metro network and they provide an increased accessibility of the public transport system. Its feeder services, long-distance services and commercial services operate on different scales of the transport system. However, like other forms of paratransit that exist in developed and developing countries, they face problems coming from lack of regulation and political integration. From our on-site investigation and in-depth interviews in Shanghai, integrating shuttle services into an overall urban transportation system implies a systematic transformation. Facilitating inter-modality is a key dimension of such a change. Consequently, public authority has an essential role to play in the development of community-based transport; transportation and urban planning departments, local and national public institutions should work together to create a new institutional framework, establish rules and create the regulatory system for the operation of shared shuttles. As a flexible, adaptive and community-based service, shared shuttles could support the development of sustainable mobility in China. With the necessary public support, they could become part of a renewed public transportation system in Chinese cities.

References

Auer, B. (2012), 'Intermodal transport - key factors for a successful cooperation of sustainable transport modes', Proceedings of Velo-City Global 2012 Conference, Vancouver. Available from: <http://www.ecf.com/wp-content/uploads/Auer-Barbara-Intermodal-Transport-Key-Factors-for-a-Successful-Cooperation____.pdf>. [March, 28 2015].

Cervero, R. and Golub, A. (2007), 'Informal Transport: A Global Perspective', Transport Policy, 14, 445-457.

Cervero, R. (1997), Paratransit in America: Redefining Mass Transportation, Praeger, Westport.

Department for Transport (2005), Review of voluntary transport: Main report. Available from: <http://webarchive.nationalarchives.gov.uk/20121107103953/http://dft.gov.uk/transport foryou/access/voluntary/reviewofvoluntarytransportma6171.html>. [March, 28 2015].

Doulet, J.-F. (2005), 'La mobilité urbaine en Chine', L'information géographique, 69, 1, 55-65.

European Commission (2004), Towards Passenger Intermodality in the EU. Analysis of the Key Issues for Passenger Intermodality Report 1. Available from: <http://www.urtp.ro/old/engl/proiecte/Passenger%20Intermodality%20Briefing%20Paper.pdf>. [March, 28 2015].

Fei, M. (2001), 'Owners Committee and China's Civil Society', Journal of ECUST (Social Science Edition), 62, 2, 57-64.

Feng, S. and Li, Q. (2013), 'Car Ownership Control in Chinese Mega Cities: Shanghai, Beijing and Guangzhou', Journey, 40-49.

Goethal, S. (2011), 'How to Integrate Current Decentralized Concentration and Urban Mobility Management? The Influence of Interactions between Urban and Transportation Planning through the Transforming Structures Of Chinese Big Cities', Proceedings of 47th ISOCARP Congress. Available from: <http://www.isocarp.net/data/case_studies/1888.pdf>. [March, 28 2015].

Hua, T. and Xu, M. (2002), 'Analysis of Shanghai's Suburbanisation', Modern Urban Research, 17, 4, 27-31.

Firnkorn, J. and Müller, M. (2012), 'Selling Mobility instead of Cars: New Business Strategies of Automakers and the Impact on Private Vehicle Holding', Business Strategy and the Environment, 21, 4, 264-280.

Ken, G. (2007), Developing the Public Transport Sector in China, World Bank, Washington DC. Available from: <http://www-wds.worldbank.org/external/default/WDSContent-Server/WDSP/IB/2010/09/17/000356161_20100917034841/Rendered/PDF/566470WP00Box31portoSectoroinoChina.pdf>. [March, 28 2015].

Kirby, R.F., Bhatt, K.U., Kemp, M.A., McGillivray, R.G. and Wohl, M. (1974), Para-transit. Neglected options for urban mobility, The Urban Institute, Washington DC.

Sioul, L., Morency, C. and Trepanier, M. (2013), 'How Carsharing Affects the Travel Behavior of Households: A Case Study of Montreal, Canada', International Journal of Sustainable Transportation, 7, 1, 52-69.

Pan, H. (2012), 'Super structure Design for Shanghai's Urban Transport Policy', Urban Planning Forum, 199, 1, 102-106.

Pan, H. (2011), Implementing Sustainable Urban Travel Policies in China, International Transport Forum, Discussion Paper No. 2011–12. Available from: <http://www.internationaltransportforum.org/jtrc/DiscussionPapers/DP201112.pdf>. [March, 28 2015].

Pan, H. and Doulet J.-F. (2010), 'The emergence of mobility services in urban China', China City Planning Review, 4, 28-31

Rathery, A. (1979), 'Les transports semi-collectifs: l'approche européenne du "paratransit"', Transports, 246, 377-386.

Schalekamp, H. and Behrens, R. (2010), 'Engaging paratransit on public transport reform initiatives in South Africa: A critique of policy and an investigation of appropriate engagement approaches', Research in Transportation Economics, 29, 371–378.

Schiller, P.L., Bruun, E.C. and Kenworthy, J.R. (2010), An Introduction to Sustainable Transportation: Policy, Planning, and Implementation, Earthscan, London/Washington DC.

Tang, L. and Liu, Q. (2010), 'Neighbourhood Carpool Practice: A Case Study on Community Carpool', Urban Transport of China, 8, 4, 29-33.

About The Journal of Sustainable Mobility

THE JOURNAL OF SUSTAINABLE MOBILITY (*JSM*) is a peer-reviewed journal that provides an interdisciplinary forum for the exchange of innovative and empirically sound research on sustainable transportation. The centrality of the journal is the sustainable developments of the automotive industry and road transport management systems, though research on other transport modes such as aviation and shipping contribute to our understanding of the future of sustainable mobility as a whole. To address the economic, environmental and societal concerns of the development of the transportation industry, the journal will take a transdisciplinary and holistic approach to gain a better understanding of the technologies that underlie the advancement of low-carbon vehicles, market demands for such vehicles, institutional change and corporate sustainability which determine the strategies of those businesses involved.

The journal focuses on aspects of green mobility in the context of nature, enterprise and technology. In particular, it aims to explore the links between transportation, technological management and innovation, energy use, sustainable development and responsible business, presenting academic research alongside practical application in order to inform policy and practice.

The *Journal of Sustainable Mobility* publishes on topics including, but not limited to, the following:

- Low-carbon vehicles technologies
- Renewable/clean/green technologies
- Biofuels and other sources of renewable energy
- Transportation management systems
- Vehicle emission controls
- Sustainable transport policies and governance
- Corporate sustainability
- Historical review of the automotive and oil industries and transport management systems
- Comparative studies of national and regional approaches to technology development and environmental control
- Case studies of innovations in technology, business models, and policy initiatives in relation to sustainable mobility

JSM is published twice annually and includes peer-reviewed papers by leading researchers, policy debate, case studies, and research notes, from Social Sciences and Engineering and Technology disciplines. It also includes reviews of the latest works published in sustainable mobility. Theme issues based on sector or region will be regularly presented. We welcome contributions from academics with a research-orientation and also business practitioners and policymakers, from the public and private sectors. *JSM* aims to be the premier journal to publish articles on sustainable mobility that accomplish an integration of theory and practice. We want the journal to be read as much by practitioners leading sustainable transport as it is by academics seeking sound research and scholarship.

JSM is essential reading for academics, practitioners, policy-makers and others interested in the latest research and thinking on sustainable transport and mobility.

JSM is published in association with Nottingham Trent University, UK, Cranfield University, UK, and the University of Chinese Academy of Sciences, China.

The *Journal of Sustainable Mobility* is included in both the Sustainable Organization Library (SOL) collection and in the smaller Greenleaf Online Library (GOL). See www.gseresearch.com/sol for further information.

EDITOR-IN-CHIEF

Dr Michael Zhang, Reader in International Strategy at Nottingham Business School, Nottingham Trent University, UK. Email: michael.zhang@ntu.ac.uk

Notes for Contributors

SUBMISSIONS

All content should be submitted via online submission. For more information see the journal homepage at www.greenleaf-publishing.com/jsm.

The form gives prompts for the required information and asks authors to submit the full text of the paper, including the title, author name and author affiliation, as a Word attachment. **Abstract and keywords will be completed via the online submission and are not necessary on the attachment.**

As part of the online submission authors will be asked to tick a box to state they have read and adhere to the Greenleaf–GSE Copyright Guidelines and have permission to publish the paper, including all figures, images, etc which have been taken from other sources. It is the author's responsibility to ensure this is correct.

In order to be able to distribute papers published in Greenleaf journals, we need signed transfer of copyright from the authors. We are committed to a liberal and fair approach to copyright and accessibility, and do not restrict authors' rights to reuse their own work for personal use or in an institutional repository.

A brief autobiographical note should be supplied at the end of the paper including:

- Full name
- Affiliation
- Email address
- Full international contact details

Please supply (via online submission) an **abstract outlining the title, purpose, methodology and main findings**. It's worth considering that, as your paper will be located and read online, the quality of your abstract will determine whether readers go on to access your full paper. We recommend you place particular focus on the impact of your research on further research, practice or society. What does your paper contribute?

In addition, please provide up to **six descriptive keywords**.

FORMATTING YOUR PAPER

Headings should be short and in bold text, with a clear and consistent hierarchy.

Please identify **Notes or Endnotes** with consecutive numbers, enclosed in square brackets and listed at the end of the article.

Figures and other images should be submitted as .jpeg (.jpg) or .tif files and be of a high quality. Please number consecutively with Arabic numerals and mark clearly within the body of the text where they should be placed.

If images are not the original work of the author, it is the author's responsibility to obtain written consent from the copyright holder to them being used. Authors will be asked to confirm this is the case by ticking the box on the online submission to say they have read and understood the Greenleaf–GSE copyright policy. Images which are neither the authors' own work, nor are accompanied by such permission will not be published.

Tables should be included as part of the manuscript, with relevant captions.

Supplementary data can be appended to the article, using the form and should follow the same formatting rules as the main text.

References to other publications should be complete and in Harvard style, e.g. (Jones, 2011) for one author, (Jones and Smith, 2011) for two authors and (Jones *et al.*, 2011) for more than two authors. A full reference list should appear at the end of the paper.

- For **books**: Surname, Initials (year), *Title of Book*, Publisher, Place of publication.
  e.g. Author, J. (2011), *This is my book*, Publisher, New York, NY.
- For **book chapters**: Surname, Initials (year), "Chapter title", Editor's Surname, Initials, *Title of Book*, Publisher, Place of publication, pages (if known).
- For **journals**: Surname, Initials (year), "Title of article", *Title of Journal*, volume, number, pages.
- For **conference proceedings**: Surname, Initials (year), "Title of paper", in Surname, Initials (Ed.), Title of published proceeding which may include place and date(s) held, Publisher, Place of publication, Page numbers.
- For **newspaper articles**: Surname, Initials (year) (if an author is named), "Article title", *Newspaper*, date, pages.
- For **images**:
  Where image is from a printed source—as for books but with the page number on which the image appears.
  Where image is from an online source—Surname, Initials (year), Title, Available at, Date accessed.
  Other images—Surname, Initials (year), Title, Name of owner (person or institution) and location for viewing.

To discuss ideas for contributions, please contact the Editor-in-Chief: Dr Michael Zhang, Reader in International Strategy at Nottingham Business School, Nottingham Trent University, UK; email: michael.zhang@ntu.ac.uk